Infinite Distraction

Theory Redux

Roberto Esposito, Persons and Things
Srećko Horvat, The Radicality of Love

Infinite Distraction
Paying Attention to Social Media

Dominic Pettman

polity

First published in 2016 by Polity Press
Reprinted 2016, 2017

Polity Press
65 Bridge Street
Cambridge CB2 1UR, UK

Polity Press
350 Main Street
Malden, MA 02148, USA

ISBN-13: 978–1–5095–0226–4
ISBN-13: 978–1–5095–0227–1(pbk.)

A catalogue record for this book is available from the British Library.

Library of Congress Cataloging-in-Publication Data

Pettman, Dominic.
  Infinite distraction / Dominic Pettman.
      pages cm
  Includes bibliographical references and index.
  ISBN 978-1-5095-0226-4 (hardback) -- ISBN 978-1-5095-0227-1 (pbk.)
  1. Distraction (Philosophy) 2. Social media. 3. Critical theory. I. Title.
  B105.D58P48 2015
  302.23'1--dc23
                                                             2015019466
              Typeset in 12.5 on 15 Adobe Garamond Pro by
              Servis Filmsetting Ltd, Stockport, Cheshire
         Printed and bound in the United States by LSC Communications

For further information on Polity, visit our website:
politybooks.com

Contents

Acknowledgments

This book would not exist were it not for Laurent de Sutter and his keen editorial eye. It was he who plucked one of my all-too-frequent Facebook updates from the digital torrent and suggested that I turn it into a focused polemic for his new book series. Laurent has been an excellent respondent to my work and staunch champion of its idiosyncrasies, for which I'm exceedingly grateful. Thanks are also due to John Thompson, who welcomed me to the postmodern *polis* of Polity with great hospitality. It was John who encouraged me to "take a position" rather than perform the usual academic labors from an imagined, highly abstract, Archimedean point. Thanks also to Neil de Cort and the editorial team at Polity for helping to usher this book into the world with such efficiency, good humor, and grace. Margret Grebowicz provided consistently brilliant feedback to my sometimes stumbling thinking around these topics. Eugene Thacker has helped me glimpse a darkly utopian world beyond, or perhaps simply before, social media. And Merritt Symes, as always, is my precious partner in various hedonic diversions within the unfoldings of daily life.

It would take several pages to personally thank all those people (colleagues, students, friends, and virtual "friends") who have enriched my micro-moments with all manner of distractions, both via the screen and in person. So I simply offer this book to my own private multitude as a perverse form of gratitude for such.

Preface:
There Is Nothing Outside the Texting

This book began its life as a humble Facebook update. In terms of media ecology and technological evolution, this is a bit like starting with a bird and ending up with a dinosaur. Despite being a professor of culture and media—that is, a professional skeptic of technological promises and practices—I certainly surrender an inordinate amount of my time interacting online in social media spaces. For fellow critic Jonathan Crary, this is no doubt in part because I—like everyone else—am obliged to submit to "mandatory techniques of digital personalization and self-administration" (43). But I would be lying if I pretended that mediated socialization doesn't bring me many micro-pleasures, along with generous infusions of exasperation, boredom, and spleen. Moreover, I would have trouble denying the fact that for every intellectual observation I post or link to, I upload several more frivolous or trivial info-morsels, designed more to distract than instruct or edify. If accused of wasting time or procrastinating, I can certainly use my job as an alibi. "Know your enemy." But the truth is that having a critical-theoretical perspective on something does not necessarily make you immune to it. An intellectual understanding of a problem does not prevent an affective investment in the same (as we all know, from our romantic histories as much as from our credit card receipts).

The following pages explore some of the more troubling effects of what we might call "the digitalization of distraction," along with its luminous shadow: attention. This book therefore touches upon some of the specific technological, cultural, social, and political constellations that solicit these two intimately connected phenomena. From anecdotes concerning common or garden-variety distractions to official reports of acute clinical cases of ADHD, there is a strong tendency to blame technology for a perceived pandemic of preoccupation. Indeed, "the media" has often been painted as little more than a distraction machine, engineered for what the curmudgeonly critic Theodor Adorno rather patronizingly called "the cross-eyed transfixion with amusement." For teachers like myself, distraction is our nemesis, just as attention is our lifeblood. Given the disheartening state of the world today, however—from terrorism to disease to corruption to exploitation to injustice to inequality to ecological catastrophe—we are likely to feel a pang of conscience at *obliging* young people to pay attention. The more we notice about the way the world works, the more we are likely to feel a crippling combination of fury, resentment, depression, shame, and helplessness. This is certainly one reason why social media is so addictive: the new opium of the masses. It dulls the pain. It screens out the screams of those suffering just outside our personal experience (or indeed the screams in our own head, on a particularly bad day). Certainly, a lot of our problems are not necessarily curable by better economic or social policies. Much of the trauma comes with being human, and thus being burdened with the awareness of mortality and other miserable fates that await us. "Being unable to cure death, wretchedness and ignorance," wrote

Pascal, "we have decided, in order to be happy, not to think about such things." Social media helps us *not* to think about such things. So there is already an irony in trying to think through and about social media.

Something else to note from the outset: social media is not a thing, or a place, or a new medium. It is a constellation, a concept. It is a virtual, evolving assemblage of elements, including—and especially—older forms of media, now dia-grammed in novel articulations. We should thus not make the mistake of reifying "it" into a stable object, even as it seeks to reify us in many ways, as well as our interactions. Just as Guy Debord's notion of the Spectacle did not simply denote the sum total of images circling in the postwar mediascape, but also expressed the ways in which we now think in and relate via images embed-ded deep in our heads, "social media" names the simultaneously limitless and circumscribed ways we interact via newly enmeshed communications and entertainment technologies. *Limitless* because no two people will navigate the same branching pathways social media affords in the same way (we all have a unique combination of interests and interactions), and *circumscribed* because these are all conducted within the vectors provided by those (increasingly few) entities that own the cables, the satellites, the channels, the sites, the providers, and the applications that funnel us all toward each other, so that we may congregate in the bright light of voluntary and compliant commerce. (Today we find a strong preference for economic commerce over the social kind—although marketers have recently realized that you can stimulate the former by simulating the latter.)

To be clear, there is no sense in simply demonizing social media, because there is no single *there* there. What I want to do, however, is focus on a troubling tendency within new modes of communication, which often goes under the name of social media. As a consequence, this is not a critique of social media, which would be akin to a critique of society *qua* technology. Rather, it is a critique of "social media" in the sense that very many companies would like to trademark that term. That is, in its narrow, shorthand sense, which points offstage to a whole industry of meshing mechanisms carefully calibrated to narrow our focus, clip our capacity for sustained attention, and shepherd as many of us as possible into the interactive sphere of reflexive consumption.

The sheer, asymptotic, never-delivered promise of the media flow demands a compulsive refresh of our screens. Real time is the new temporal standard. Enormous amounts of energy are expended for everything to be streaming live, so that we are not stranded in the past, in history, in the archive, where we might gather dust (or actually learn something). If you dare lift your eyes from the screen even for a moment, you might miss the tweet or the post or the update that promises to change your life. Links are assumed to have a lifespan of only a few days, if that. Everything is in flux. And yet each day feels the same as the one before.

These days, to adapt Heraclitus, you never step in the same live stream twice.

And yet the digital river is tediously familiar.

"You shall know them by their fruits," Jesus says in Matthew 7:16. From the point of view of the world we share in common, the fruits in question are altogether tasteless. I have seen young teenagers who just yesterday were ebullient, verbal, interactive, and full of personality turn into aphasic zombies within three months of getting a smart phone or an iPad. The new wine is dying on the vine, and Dionysos, the telluric god of ecstasy, is nowhere in sight. It is unlikely that the next big digital innovation will lure him back.

Robert Pogue Harrison, "The Children of Silicon Valley"

Let us avoid making a Gothic novel, as well as a romance, out of information technology.

Henri Lefebvre, *Critique of Everyday Life*

Introduction

I Know Why the Caged Bird Tweets

We will have to suffer this new state of things, this forced extroversion of all interiority, this forced injection of all exteriority.

Jean Baudrillard, "The Ecstasy of Communication"

In the waning days of 2014, Instagram purged its accounts of billions of bots—automated, fake user accounts—so that a slew of celebrities woke up with several million fewer followers than they had when they went to sleep. It was a vicious purge, under the cover of darkness. No doubt tears were shed that same morning, and some agents started looking for a new high-profile client. Were we ourselves not flawed humans but particularly sympathetic bots, this code-induced holocaust may have sounded like the destruction of the planet Alderaan to Obi-Wan Kenobi in *Star Wars*: "I felt a great disturbance in the Force, as if millions of voices suddenly cried out in terror, and were suddenly silenced. I fear something terrible has happened." In my own case, however, I noticed no difference, since I have an Instagram account with zero followers. I use this account to post selfies for the exclusive pleasure of the network's blind, unblinking eye. Why? Because I am amused by the very existence of a social media account with no followers whatsoever, no actual *social* component. And yet, as the existence of bots makes clear, once uploaded to the network, no posting goes "unread" or "unseen," in some form or another, even if only under the obscure heading of "metadata."

Which leads to the question: to what degree are humans different from bots when it comes to the various metrics concerning online behavior? To what extent have our own routines become fully preempted *sub*routines, or apparently algorithmic? From a certain angle—say, the angle of Target's commercial recommendation engine—a woman can now be assumed to be pregnant on the basis of a series of word searches in Google or some adjustments in shopping habits. The corporation presumes to know this information, perhaps even before the mother-to-be has realized it herself (as happened in one high-profile case). The vast nano-army of harvesting functions that help amass "big data" read the digital tea leaves for patterns in which we ourselves seem to dissolve as individuals (at least until such time as the authorities have a vested interest in fishing our unique personage out of the electronic soup; *then* the individual is suddenly reconstituted from the morass).

This is where we find ourselves, a decade and a half into the twenty-first century: suspended between bot and not, between anonymous and tagged, generic and specific. We hover between the older conceptions of what it is to be a person—a *citizen*, with rights, responsibilities, character, agency, identity, and so on—and new, emerging types of being—a *consumer*, with cravings, likes, profiles, and opinions, leaving a trail of cookie crumbs in our wake. Today, the sovereign individual of liberal philosophy and history is rather rapidly morphing into what Gilles Deleuze called the "dividual": that is, the sub-subject of a more modular ontology, better designed for connection to flexible assemblages (themselves designed for a world based less on the transcendental "I" than the transnational Ikea).

Or so the story goes.

There is certainly no shortage of polemics out there, pleading with us to stop "clicking ourselves to death," to stop using the unprecedented reach and power of the Internet to distract ourselves from the late capitalist conspiracy to suck what's left of our souls, our bodies, our bank accounts, and everything of value in the environment, whether it be the interactions we have online or the minerals that are mined in order to make our communications gadgets in the first place. Every new technology brings with it a new McLuhan, a new Toffler, a new Postman, or a new Turkle, warning us against the dangers of the reflex adoption of new cybernetic arrangements, which themselves form the contours of new modes of cultural and political compliance. Indeed, the present book is not immune from such admonishments. It does, however, seek to do more than add yet another concerned voice to the Neo-Luddite Choir, by tracing some of the ways in which the public social critique of

"the Media" (if we can even talk in such monolithic terms anymore) is often itself fed back
into the very same overcoded circuits to better
increase its reach, efficiency, and profit margins.
Moreover, along the way, this short book seeks
to identify some of the ways in which new media
platforms bring unexpected social possibilities
as well as politically progressive agendas to the
table, even as they foreclose on other, more tried
and true orientations or arrangements. (Such an
approach to technological change falls under the
sign of "the *pharmakon*," at least since Plato—a
"remedy" with the capacity for both curing and
killing the user, and thus to be approached with
caution.)

Jean Baudrillard is an interesting figure, in this
sense, and still the most prescient diagnostician
of the radical fracture or revolution that occurred
with the rise of the simulated society. While
he is usually read as a pessimist, in the post–
Frankfurt School tradition ("things may not have
been better before, but they are certainly getting worse!"), he would at times insist that he is
not simply lamenting these anomalous develop-
ments, since they are too vast and swift to account
for as yet. In his classic short work "The Ecstasy

of Communication," Baudrillard argues that subjectivity itself has lost its "scene," the traditional site of its genesis and drama, and has instead been replaced by the "*ob*scene": a nowhere-land of screens and informatics. Where the original scene was essentially psychological (based on such key distinctions as private vs. public, self vs. other, subject vs. object), the new obscenity is not interested in such a congealed metaphysics, with its reassuring markers of difference and dialectical *agon*. Thanks to "the narcissistic and protean era of connections" (127), the mirror is replaced by the network: a decisive substitution, leading to a very different way of being human (many would say, to a mode of being posthuman, more in tune with the machine). Gone are the melancholic missed encounters of self-reflection, along with the generative struggles for recognition. In their place appears "a nonreflecting surface . . . where operations unfold—the smooth operational surface of communication" (126–27). The result?

No more expenditure, consumption, performance, but instead regulation, well-tempered functionality, solidarity among all the elements of the same system, control and global management of an ensemble. . . . Private "telematics": each person sees himself at the controls of a hypothetical machine, isolated in a position of perfect and remote sovereignty, at an infinite distance from his universe of origin. Which is to say, in the exact position of an astronaut in his capsule, in a state of weightlessness that necessitates a perpetual orbital flight and a speed sufficient to keep him from crashing back to his planet of origin. (128)

It is remarkable to think that this description was offered in a time before the World Wide Web gave mass-access to the Internet and its various hubs and clusters. Certainly, this portrait of the orbital, telematic subject is not so different from Sherry Turkle's recent account of the digital age, in which we find ourselves "alone together": floating trapped in an uncanny and unsettling kind of networked solipsism. (A rather straightforward varnish on the prewar critique of the movie palace as a shrine for secular "lonely crowds.") For Turkle, the stakes are still wagered within a paradigm of *alienation*. By this account, the constant solicitation of the Internet estranges us from our authentic selves, because we no longer foster each other's welfare in the irreplaceable face-to-face community (the *locus classicus* of Humanity 1.0, which anthropologist Robin Dunbar tells us cannot grow beyond 150 or so members, without losing cohesion). We have thus traded in "real" relationships for simulated ones, like the willingly deluded character in *The Matrix* who is content with digital steak, as long as it tastes real to his inherently mediated mind and tastebuds. For Baudrillard, however, such a post-Edenic narrative is already compromised by its romantic sense of human history, where alienation is still possible (and thus, so is *transcending* alienation, and at least in theory, toward a more genuine mode of existence). For the more cynical Frenchman, "We are no longer a part of the drama of alienation; we live in the ecstasy of communication. And this ecstasy is obscene" (130).

Ecstasy comes from the Greek word *ek-stasis*— to be outside of oneself. Perhaps this *externalizing* aspect of communication explains the allure of social media, even for those who profess to despise it. (We all know some of those solitary heroes who refuse to join Facebook or Twitter or Instagram; as fascinating in their self-discipline or willful anachronism as they are vexing in their stubborn Bartlebyesque refusal to "get with the

8

program.") Ecstatic technologies suggest that Sartre had it the wrong way around, and hell is in fact *ourselves*. Or rather, he had it half-right. Hell is ourselves, yes. It is other people, too. And it is also the *complete absence* of other people. So we have obliged ourselves to fashion an enormous infrastructure to keep people beyond arm's length, away from our actual space, but not so far that we suffer from the lack of reassuring, telegraphic signals of companionship. We want to have it both ways: to be distracted from our own failings and to-do lists, while being simultaneously relieved of the kind of exhausting obligation evoked by the presence and needs of the actual other—those same obligations that, for at least several millennia, went, until recently, under the name of "society."

But again, such rhetoric risks lapsing into possibly obsolete categories: the psychological, the alienated, the *scene*. As we well know, this "ecstasy" afforded by social media is decidedly not an overwhelming thrill or sense of bliss, but rather the homeopathic parceling of tiny and banal moments of recognition, reassurance, ego reinforcement, humblebragging, notoriety, curiosity, shame, and a galaxy of other modest—but collectively significant—affects. What remains is a type of subjectivity susceptible to psychological issues and symptoms, but without the psychoanalytic scaffolding which hitherto reinforced the biological skeleton of the self. So we are still narcissistic, but in a convex sense, reflecting out to the network rather than into the whirlpools of our own pupils. (We are becoming "exo-subjects," sending selfies out into the void, in the search for validation of a self that is now distributed across the wires.) According to this reasoning, our own expropriating experiences of the network augur a new species: self-obsessed yet without a workable sense or definition of selfhood.[1] Which itself adds up to a society without the social.

But this rhetoric also discounts the many different contexts for using social media: on holiday, grounded in one's bedroom, goofing off at work, while held under arrest, and so on. Such situations in themselves often explain "why the caged bird tweets"—out of boredom, loneliness, desperation, urgency, or ADD. There is certainly a compulsive, addictive, more-ish cycle to social media use. (We also all know those people who deactivate, and then reactivate, their accounts as regularly as they do their laundry.) We have a seemingly insatiable appetite for distraction. But distraction from what?

One of the assumptions of this book is that distraction itself has mutated, as a phenomenon, strategy, and geometric figure. Distraction is no longer a gesturing *away from* that which disturbs, or that which others do not want noticed. It is not to "create a distraction" so that something else may slip by or remain unconfronted. Rather, the decoy itself—the thing designed to distract—has merged with the distraction imperative, so that, for instance, news coverage of race riots now *distracts* from the potential reality and repercussions of race riots. This is a more sophisticated form of propaganda than those engineered in the twentieth century, when the conscious decision would be made to distract from civil rights protests by screening the Miss America Pageant. This new form of distraction—which acknowledges as much as it disavows—is harder to mobilize against, for the simple reason that no one can accuse "the media" of trying to cover up "the truth." Rather, incessant and deliberately framed representations of events are *themselves* used to obscure and muffle those very same events.[2]

This adds a "meta" element to our own attempts to distract ourselves from the world's, and our own, problems. Social media can allow for escapism. But it can also amplify the things we would ideally like to escape from. Hence, the ouroboric aspect of online interactivity—a snake eating its own tail. We distract ourselves from the network's incapacity to (fully) distract. And yet, one more click might just do the trick! As Baudrillard cannily notes, "The promiscuity that reigns over the communication networks is one of superficial saturation, of an incessant solicitation, of an extermination of interstitial and protective spaces. . . . Speech is free perhaps, but I am less free than before: I no longer succeed in knowing what I want, the space is so saturated, the pressure so great from all who want to make themselves heard" (131–32). For Baudrillard (and others), the subject is no longer paranoid or melancholic, but schematically schizophrenic. The fascination of the network is "pure . . . aleatory and psychotropic." Given the ecstatic nature of such pleasures, the subject "can no longer produce the limits of his own being, can no longer play nor stage himself, can no longer produce himself as mirror. He is now only a pure screen, a switching center for all the networks of influence" (133). The degree to which we see ourselves in such a portrait probably depends on whether we consider this a dystopian vision or a potentially liberating threshold: the chrysalis for a post-humanist type of humanity.

Baudrillard considered "the masses" to be subversive by their very herd- or swarm-like behavior, by their stubborn refusal to participate in a legible way. "They do not radiate," he writes; "on the contrary, they absorb all radiation from the outlying constellations of State, History, Culture, Meaning. They are inertia, the strength of inertia, the strength of the neutral" (*In the Shadow* 2). Given how effectively we have volunteered to be a part of the clicksphere, one wonders if he would be quite so impressed with the masses, now that they can be data-mined with such exquisite detail. Baudrillard's masses were the "silent majority" of television watchers and couch potatoes. But TV could not, at that time, track your eyeball movements, eavesdrop on your conversations, and invite you to purchase product-placements in real time. We now shed information about ourselves at the same rate as skin cells or strands of hair, to be vacuumed up by some of the same bots that were sacrificed in the line of duty at the beginning of this chapter. Then again, the more macro the data, the more opaque these "selves" become, when scaled down to the level of the solitary user. The more information the marketing machines collect about "us," the less a coherent narrative emerges. (Or what emerges is a narrative so simple it tells us next to nothing.) The signal becomes distorted out of any shape in the attendant noise. Perhaps the masses will have the last laugh after all, but only on this scale of the multitude. Taken one by one, our much-vaunted "quality of life" is still severely compromised by the new synchronizing systems.

Such are the various grids to consider when attempting to intervene in the torrent of commentary on social media. The very decision to write "a book" about interactive networks presumes the capacity to manufacture an object somewhat removed from that milieu, in order to have the necessary distance and perspective to write about it (even as the book is likely to end up as a pdf file online soon after publication). The challenge of doing so is connected to the incentive, obliging us to contend with the manifold contexts in which these practices occur, inscribe themselves, and, in turn, reconfigure their own relations. Just out of frame, but informing every word, pulses the *political economy* surrounding social media: the types of gray-market labor, environmental exploitation, neocolonial sweat-shops, legalized corruption, financial coercion, and cynical deployment of desiring machines that produce the gadgets, the infrastructure, and the parasitical applications that inhabit it. Firmly within the frame will be the so-called *attention economy*: the different ways in which "eyeballs" or "brainshare" represents the means, as well as the ends, for much cultural activity in the new millennium. Indeed, some recent observers have argued that we are in fact more enmeshed in an attention *ecology*; a hypothesis taken seriously in the following pages, given the emphasis on distraction (and thus its opposite). One recent structural condition to consider from the outset is the decisive erosion of the online/offline distinction, thanks in large part to mobile devices, which means that we can no longer speak in confident terms of the virtual in contrast to the actual.

In terms of possible methodologies, there are the various disciplinary approaches: ethnography, psychology, evolutionary biology, neuroscience, sociology, history, philosophy, and so on—each as valid as the other for something as complex and perplexing as new media (and each as blinkered as the other when considered only through its own set of optics). One could certainly take the counter-intuitive "cultural studies" approach and celebrate the quotidian micro-resistances of bloggers, tumblers, tweeters, and the like, emphasizing the diagonal agency or provisional empowerment of personal testimonials. Or, in sharp contrast, one could paint the entire user base of the Internet as manipulated dupes: the broad critical brushstrokes swirling into a pop-art mural called, "What Would Adorno Say?" This book flirts promiscuously with many of these possible approaches, so that it may better assemble a strategic suite of perspectives to bear on the complex articulations between distraction and social media. The intent is not to provide the definitive crystallized account of the network condition. Nor is it to offer a more nuanced corrective to some of the more influential laments about the direction our technologies are taking us. Instead, it seeks to isolate some key symptomatic points of convergence between rhetoric, technics, and praxis, in order to test the hypothesis that our

16

appetite for distraction originates not simply in some timeless human flaw or metaphysical condition, but also, and especially, within the historically specific—and thus contingent—political determinations of (and limitations on) our communicational options.

As Simone Weil once wrote, attention is "the rarest and purest form of generosity" (in Vetö 45). It could be said, then, that Weil is thus an "attention-seeker," in the non-pejorative sense of someone who searches for an uncommon and much-needed *capacity*—a capacity to create worlds by acknowledging them into existence. Strangely, the most effective way to discourage the precious and enriching resource of attention is not, as one might suppose, by distracting via an all-purpose decoy. It is not by ensuring we are all preoccupied with the same ultimately meaning-less "water cooler" pseudo-event (effective as this may be on its own terms). Rather, those with a vested interest in minimizing critical, deep, and/or long-lasting attention have figured out carefully crafted ways to do so. Indeed, these same people are paid astronomical sums in order to keep us "looking at the bunny" with ever more ingenious click bait. And no matter how conscious we are of this process—in being aware of their tricks at the same rate they can produce them—we are still vulnerable to their solicitations and seductions. Why? Because we are creatures who, above all, need to communicate (*homo communis*). So when it comes to the *consumers* of the means of communication, affect trumps knowledge. This is why we may curse Zuckerberg's name yet continue to click around Facebook. We go in search of the trigger for a milligram of diluted dopamine, and in doing so generate yet more revenue for this company, whose business model is based on offering a "reasonable facsimile" of company itself. When it comes to the *owners* of the means of communication, however, knowledge trumps affect, precisely because the former emerges from the latter, in monetized form. The PowerPoint Posse have figured out how to incite, tickle, and channel fleeting feelings into reliable revenue streams.

From one angle, this puts us all on "the same page" of Zuckerberg's ubiquitous "book" (to the extent that the Facebook empire extends far beyond his own servers).[3] But from another angle, this "synchronization" of souls, forged through new, global technologies, is in fact somewhat *out* of sync when viewed up close. In other words, the system deploys its resources and specifically tailored protocols, to synchronize our squirrel-like attention spans. At the same time, it is doing something less Orwellian, but perhaps even more sinister: tweaking and modulating our increasingly homogeneous gaze into staggered or delayed micro-experiences. Social media may *seem* to be the space that constantly synchronizes a billion smooth discussions, unfolding "in real time." But such interactions are in fact stuttering, like a streaming movie in which the moving lips don't quite match the sound. The things we "share" online do not arrive "in time," in one piece, or in the manner they were intended. The promise embedded in the name Instagram, that *différance* can be abolished, can never be kept. But of course, this just motivates us to share more and more "content," in the rather manic hope it will one day arrive at its destination. (Lacan might well have said, "There is no social [media] relationship.")

What happens to a world in which distraction becomes the rule rather than an exception? Indeed, what happens to a world in which distraction is the very motor of its economy, both commercial and libidinal? For those critics aligned in hindsight with the Frankfurt School and its largely Marxist perspective on popular culture, distraction was not reduced to a moral hazard, but considered a complex cultural symptom as well as a novel social phenomenon, charged with enormous political potential. Siegfried Kracauer, for instance, writing between the wars, viewed the Berlin picture palace as ground-zero for distraction. But he did not focus on "the cult of distraction" to dismiss this new technological shrine, and its attendant rituals of consumption, as something irretrievably frivolous. Rather, the movie theater served to collapse the already fragile distinction between "the masses" and "the educated classes," creating instead "the *homogeneous cosmopolitan audience*," in which "everyone has the *same* responses, from the bank director to the sales clerk, from the diva to the stenographer" (325). For Kracauer, as for Walter Benjamin, film was a new form of democratized and mechanized art that shatters all previous modes of aesthetic reception and contemplation. "The stimulations of the senses succeed one another with such rapidity that there is no room left between them for even the slightest contemplation" (326). The spectator in the cinema has little choice but to be distracted by the film itself, since there is no opportunity to form one's own reflective opinion. One is simply seized, arrested, mesmerized, and absorbed—leading to a new type of mass distraction.

We might ask, then, who is the subject of distraction? And what is this subject being distracted from? The answer provided by Kracauer—and others of his ilk—is that *the masses* are the collective subject undergoing an ongoing process of distraction (the masses being a new sociological entity forged in the crucible of a new social and economic reality). The mass is thus posited in relation to an unprecedented scaling-up of spectatorship, along with its many moods and modes. But what is the mass being distracted from? Again, for Kracauer, it is not simply that the owners of the picture palaces, and the bosses of the film industry, were duping the people into fantastical celluloid landscapes, in order to distract the masses from the fact that they are being alienated and exploited (although strategically deployed incentives toward escapist entertainments were certainly considered part of the equation). "In a profound sense," Kracauer writes, "Berlin audiences act truthfully when they . . . [prefer] the surface glamor of the stars, films, revues, and spectacular shows [in contrast to more traditional and sacrosanct forms of art]. Here, in pure externality, the audience encounters itself; its own reality is revealed in the fragmented sequence of splendid sense impressions. Were this reality to remain hidden from the viewers, they could neither attack nor change it; its disclosure in distraction is therefore of *moral* significance" (326). Film reveals the truth via a new form of artifice, just as poetry or tragic theater revealed something morally true through artificial means in previous epochs.

"But," Kracauer continues, with an important qualification, "this is the case *only if distraction is not an end in itself*" (emphasis added). Distraction must instead be a *means*: a means toward an empowering perspective on life, and on the way it (that is, the vitality of the people) has been captured, organized, and diminished by the invested minority. In this very deliberate definition of the term, distraction is "meaningful only as improvisation, as a reflection of the uncontrolled anarchy of our world" (327). For "one is often struck by the momentary insight that someday all this will suddenly burst apart" ("this" being the carefully staged world of relations created and maintained through the relentless production of capital). For Kracauer, "the entertainment to which the general public throngs ought to produce the same effect" (327). In other words, the new medium of film has (or, rather, *had*, at least during its first few decades) the potential to explode the sociopolitical status quo, by virtue of its disorientingly new perspective on reality, and its radical reorganization of the senses through an intensity of aesthetic effects (and affects). The problem is that the movie theater, as an anachronistically designed space of choreographed consumption, works against the destabilizing potential of the film itself. Movie theaters will not fulfill their *social* vocation, according to Kracauer, "until they aim radically toward a kind of distraction that exposes disintegration instead of masking it." The good news? "It could be done in Berlin, home of the masses—who so easily allow themselves to be stupefied *only because they are so close to the truth*" (328, emphasis added).

Kracauer's influence on Benjamin can be seen in the latter's views on distraction. In the second, "master" version of his famous "Work of Art in

the Age of Its Technological Reproducibility,"
Benjamin reiterates the ideological distinction
between the distracted masses and the *devoted* art
lover (the latter, always, tellingly, figured in the
singular): "Distraction and concentration form
an antithesis, which may be formulated as fol-
lows. A person who concentrates before a work
of art is absorbed by it; he enters into the work,
just as, according to legend, a Chinese painter
entered his completed painting while behold-
ing it. By contrast, the distracted masses absorb
the work of art into themselves. Their waves lap
around it; they encompass it with their tide"
(39–40). Benjamin's "prototype" of an artwork
that is received collectively, and in a state of distraction, is architecture, since this form of art is
experienced and inhabited through a cluster of
ambient habits produced by, and acquired from,
the human commons.

Benjamin never fully fleshed out his "Theory
for Distraction," since this languished in his desk
as a short series of notes. Yet it is here, in the idea
of architecture as "reception in distraction," that
we reconnect to social media. (For what could
be a better "prototype" of social media than
architecture?) We navigate public and private

24

buildings through various senses, and through various states of attention and preoccupation. We do the same with the digital environment. The latter is pre-diagrammed for us, by and through protocols, applications, and devices. For Benjamin, "the human apparatus of perception" functions just as much at the level of touch and habit as by vision. Thus, as if describing a twenty-first-century city dweller, ordering a café latte while texting a colleague, Benjamin writes, "even the distracted person can form habits. What is more, the ability to master certain tasks in a state of distraction first proves that their performance has become habitual" (40). Distraction is thus revealed to be a physiological phenomenon (56). And it is on the level of the body and its reflexes that we must look for the registration of new media. (Just as our bodies feel the vibrating of imagined phone messages today, like the pulsing of phantom limbs, so too the moviegoer of the 1920s and 1930s experienced the cinema.)

Distraction is thus a double-edged sword. On the one hand, it can be a specific affective state in which the subject, experienced as a member of the masses, can "get closer" to the reality of things, and thereby learn a new set of responses to the revealed world. On the other hand, this type of "simultaneous collective reception" is particularly vulnerable to being *re*-distracted *away from* the glimpsed reality; away from that-which-we-all-have-in-common, beyond our individual pinhole perspectives on life, and back into the obfuscatory phantasmagoria of commodification. Today's social media, like film in the 1920s and 1930s, promises to open windows onto a new reality, which itself could inspire a recalibration of the real conditions of social existence. But just as Kracauer saw the structure of the movie theater as containing and taming the power of the films it showed, the brands and corporations that provide us with the access to socially mediated technospaces today close such windows far faster than they can be opened. Indeed, these conglomerates create entire divisions charged with ensuring such windows remain undiscovered, or at least nailed shut from within.

Nearly a century after the German critics were identifying a new and exclusively modern form of diversion, the dialectic between explosion and control continues. Certainly, the masses continue to have a voracious appetite for distraction. And yet, we tend to forget that distraction itself is a very truncated, compromised, or uncommitted form of attention. (Or, even more radically, as Thomas Elsaesser has suggested, we forget that attention is simply *a specific type of distraction*.) To be distracted is to be "draw[n] in different directions" or "pull[ed] asunder" (OED).[4] Not too long ago it was a term for insanity. As our computing devices evolve with parallel processors, we are obliged to do the same, partitioning our brain into effective multitasking components. But of course there are organic limits, and cultural collateral damage, in attempting to upgrade ourselves at the same pace as the Apple release calendar.[5] The issue is not simply the dominant mode of distraction, but the dialectical way in which such distraction is composed of millions of tiny moments of engineered *attention* (or vice versa). Once again, the shift in focus reveals different aspects of the composition. If we observe a city dweller in a coffee shop working on a laptop, we might deduce she has Zen powers of meditation: almost autistic in her unblinking state of attention. But were we to actually look at the same screen ourselves, we are likely to find several windows open, as the user chats, toggles, switches, tweets, cuts, pastes, and emojis her way between several other similarly entranced yet antsy people. The gaze is long but shallow, different in kind to the (now almost extinct) raptured spectator in the cinema.

The designers of our apps and interfaces, fully aware of this experimental cold fusion between distraction and attention, have minted rapidly adaptive protocols for keeping the spiral going, with little care for the limits (social, biological, ecological) they test and transgress. Those dehumanizing forces, which French philosopher Bernard Stiegler has called "the program industries," have taken the profitable lessons learned by the so-called culture industries and recodified them for a digital mediascape.[6] In this mode, Stiegler talks of the insidious "hypersynchronization" afforded by contemporary technologies. By this term he means (to quote one of his translators, Patrick Crogan) "an excessive, preemptive industrial production of the collective through, above all, industrial temporal objects." Beneath the technical language, Stiegler is identifying something essential here: the unprecedented historical redefinition of "the people" *through* technologies which, at the same stroke, disenfranchise, and perhaps even erase, any collective sense of what it

28

means to be "the people." Hypersynchronization is thus about the cynical, corporate-governmental control of attention, behavior, and thought, through physiological and phantasmatic mechanisms. It directly connects to what Jonathan Crary calls "the standardization of experience" (76); that is, the deliberate staging and framing of life so that it is consumable and thus consumed. Or, in much simpler terms (and to quote Stiegler himself), hypersynchronization is "to become herd-like" ("Automatization" 70).

What if the problem, however, is not that we are all synchronized to the same affective networks and moments, but the objects of a more exquisitely sinister modulation? What if the herd is being directed into different pastures, for quite different reasons? What if the raison d'être of so-called social media is to calibrate the interactive spectacle so that we *never feel the same way* as other potential allies and affines at the same moment? In this case, it is quite deliberate that while one person is fuming about economic injustice or climate change denial, another is giggling at a cute cat video. And—two hours later—vice versa. That nebulous indignation which constitutes the very fuel of true social change can then be redirected safely around the network, in a manner akin to the energy companies with electricity around the country, avoiding any dangerous surges. So instead of "hypersynchronization," we might want to call this strategic phenomenon *hypermodulation*. Or, less of a mouthful, deliberate dissonance. Productive delay. Staggered distraction.

I

Hypermodulation
(or the Digital Mood Ring)

One of the first things to note is that the phrase
"social media" can be read as both a tautology
and an oxymoron. In the first sense, media is
understood to be inherently and essentially social,
given that we tend to call "media" any technology
or technique employed to communicate beyond
and between the atomic unit of the individual.
The phrase is thus redundant. Indeed, it is difficult to imagine what "anti-social media" might
even look like (although it could be fun to try).
In the second sense, however, we encounter the
now familiar paradox that *too* much media leads
to anti-social situations, such as the proverbial
friend or family member who would rather check
their phone than talk to the people sitting at the

same table. The social here migrates *away* from the directly interpersonal, to a simulated version with a much narrower bottleneck for giving and receiving social cues.

Social media is meant—we are told—to make us feel less alone.[7] And indeed it often does, by granting us instant and ongoing access to "the lives of others." But as historian and theorist Karl Steel notes, "When we see these thoughts in writing; when we realize that everyone in our newsfeed also has some kind of rich 'inner life'; when we have unprecedented access to other people's minds (no matter how carefully edited), we are apt to feel a stronger, *rebound* loneliness: that of knowing, now for certain, that very few people (if any) are thinking or feeling *along* with us, or in tune with us." Social media takes the guesswork out of loneliness, but not necessarily the sting (something Jonathan Crary calls "the hallucination of presence" [29]). Hence we find a dialectical tension between isolation and connection, nestled within the larger one, powered by the torque between distraction and attention. Sitting at home, or roaming the city, we spend much of our time passing around shorthand signifiers of our current emotional place on the continuum spanning hermetic contempt and abject surrender to the network. Whether we consider ourselves likers or lurkers, we no longer have to come up with phatic phrases to slap some more social glue onto our interactions, since pre-designed emojis are at hand, to help paste a cute visage on the accelerated standardization of expression. The very legibility of these tokens helps to create an index of affective mediascapes. And their hegemonic formatting enables all those various "snapshots" of the local, national, or global temper. Thanks to the magic of info-graphics, we can watch "outrage" sweep across Twitter like a forest fire. We can tag and track "anticipation"—whether this be for the release of a blockbuster film or a major sporting event—as this highly prized human resource lights up vari-ous demographically determined sectors of the social web. Heatmaps, wordmaps, issue trackers, phrase radars, hashtag trends, buzz forecasts—all combine to render our own collective "mood" in such high resolution that only Silicon Valley has the server capacity to capture and process it. Just as polls of various kinds entranced Baudrillard's ambivalent masses—so narcissistically involved with their own informational shadow that they morph to match its shape—these new digital mood rings allow an ever more complex and cus-tomizable portrait of the mercurial, monotonous Zeitgeist. Rather than simply being *reported*, as they were in the time of high broadcast televi-sion, these new polls are customizable, searchable, reconfigurable, filterable, and otherwise "oper-able." Which of course makes them all the more fascinating to us, as the permanent feedback loop of real-time data provides a four-dimensional mirror in which to catch our reflection: a mass-selfie of four billion people at once, ever changing, yet with the same frozen smile (or grimace).

And it is these same algorithmic objects which authorize and instruct the exquisite modulation that traps us in such pre-determined circuits. One profitable social media phenomenon can be rep-licated and amplified, once the right memes have been fluffed and released, the right vectors greased by the right effluvia scraped from the right viral infectors. To be sure, the system is much hap-pier if the trending topic du jour is Grumpy Cat and not a protest against Wall Street. But the latter can easily be contained so long as there are a variety of different "stories" competing for our attention. Indeed, that is the salient point here:

that matters of potentially historic import, like a civil rights issue, for instance, are now flattened into the same homogeneous, empty digital space as a cute critter or an obnoxious celebrity (and vice versa). While television was the pioneer in creating this absolute exchangeability of "events"—in order to dispense with the political charge of a real event—the "human interest" story was still quarantined from the News of the Night by coming at the end of the broadcast (just as it was relatively clear, until the past couple of decades, what was a news story and what was advertising—even as they often reinforced each other, as publicity for certain types of conduct). Now, in the new click-based configuration which makes up the interface between ourselves and *what's going on*, every story is equivalent, and thus none more meaningful than any other. We need only glance at our ever-refreshing newsfeed to see how seemingly "raw" information is in fact preprocessed at the same plant, and using the same sterilization procedures. (One particularly egregious example, stumbled upon at the time of writing, came courtesy of Facebook's "trending" panel: "1. #Ferguson: Protests continue after grand jury doesn't charge officer in Michael Brown case. 2. Paul Rudd:

University of Kansas yearbook photo shows actor sporting long hair style.")

Twitter trolls, malicious Yik Yakkers, and YouTube commentators excepted, we thankfully haven't yet reached the stage where we react to all these news niblets in the same way. We still feel appalled when we read of injustice, just as we feel heartened when we are exposed to stories of empathy and good will. But all of these contradictory signals create great confusion in our hearts and minds, not only because they come so thick and fast, but because each one is rendered equivalent to the other by virtue of its place in the Feed. To be visible on social media is to exist, at least for the fleeting flicker one is onscreen. To exist is to demand a moment of the world's time, its attention. And so we pay the coin of our desire to be informed or amused. But this necessarily leads to "cognitive dissonance": the inability to process two incompatible pieces of information. Or rather, today, in contrast to *older* modes of cognitive dissonance, social media disorients us precisely to the degree that mutually exclusive entities are rendered *all too compatible*. All the moral hierarchies of human culture crumble into a caricature of democracy, in which all elements are equal. This in turn creates an *affective* analog or parallel to our distress: an "*emotional* dissonance," forged from being pulled in different directions; charmed by videos of interspecies friendships and (almost) simultaneously disgusted by the latest crime footage released on the wires.

No doubt there are human subjects right now—probably anxious college students, hoping to lessen their debt upon graduation—being tested under lab conditions by *Clockwork Orange*–style psychologists, assaulting these young men and women with images of war, torture, misery, and violence, all intercut with cute fluffy ducklings and happy Fred Astaire dances. But we need not wait for their published findings. We are living the results of such experiments every day. We ourselves are guinea pigs who signed our mental welfare away as soon as we clicked on the interminable End User License Agreement. No wonder we feel so drained by noon, or even before we get dressed. We are being hypermodulated, our nipples tweaked, our noses turned, and our eyeballs twisted. We are being played like a giant keyboard, even as we ourselves seem to be the masterly Mozart figures, tapping on the keys and making things happen.

But it would be a mistake to think this refers to an actual conspiracy, the kind that could be reduced to an Adam Curtis narrative. (As impressive and persuasive as these are, Curtis's *grands récits* are certainly reductionist and leave out as much as they put in.) Such subplots no doubt exist, with devastating consequences. But "the system" is far too complex to be engineered or orchestrated by a small cabal—unless we call such a group the 1 percent (which is already too many people to add up to a conspiracy, at least in the traditional sense). The Koch brothers may have links to Murdoch, who may have links to the top rank at Monsanto and Blackwater, who in turn may have links, via shady off-shore companies, to the biggest players in Silicon Valley. But there is no single puppet master, or set of puppet masters. The inhibiting synchronization via modulation that constitutes the glue of social media is not authorized by the push of a button, setting the whole Rube Goldberg machine in motion. It is not a conscious decision that can be traced back to the one office, the one meeting, the one post-orgy pact. Rather, it has been sculpted by the millions of patient "invisible hands" of the market, which parallel Darwinian evolution in terms of fostering the most efficient forms for their own purposes. Only in this case, the purpose isn't "life" but "profits." The Internet of our age is an ingenious piece of "intelligent design," in which God is not Tim Berners-Lee or the Google guys, but the imperative to make money. This sounds simple enough. But it involves the consent and creativity of entire populations to make it work. By participating in our various ways—from actively writing code for new applications to enthusiastically adopting the very same—we all contribute to "the system." By answering the "ping" of a message, we add a single straw to the camel's back (just as two other people, fresh out of MIT or ITP, augment the camel's spine with reinforcing space-age materials). This conspiracy is essentially *acephalic*—headless—even as we can identify key players in its ongoing execution. No one person or group can be blamed. When the revolution comes, we'll all be obliged to line up against the wall (at least all of us who have ever gone online). Which is to say that these troubling tendencies cannot be uncoupled from the economic and ideological system within which they were born. And it would be a waste of breath to condemn any one group as "manipulators," unless we gesture in the vague direction of "the owners of the means of reproduction." The problem is, in the age of the prosumer, we are all complicit. So the question isn't who to petition (now or later), but how to begin looking for—or better yet, creating—a radically different definition of "social media."

I just referred to synchronicity-via-hypermodulation. But what do I mean by that exactly? Recall the synchronized movement of the workers in Fritz Lang's dystopian sci-fi classic *Metropolis*. This was not to be our fate (even as many factory workers indeed do repetitive mechanical tasks more or less in sync). Instead, the default motion in the overdeveloped countries is a postmodern ballet. On the one hand, we have still-life tableaux of "creatives," moving nothing but their click fingers and coffee cups. And on the other, we encounter a dramatic flurry of dynamic motion and bustling activity. (Picture an executive talking on the phone while being whisked into a helicopter.) The contrast embedded into such choreography suggests a galaxy of local differences. These discrepancies, however, ultimately add up to the same kind of homogeneity in *Metropolis*. Visually and aesthetically, they are very different. But politically (which is to say, economically) they are ultimately the same.

For Stiegler, the triumph of hypersynchronization results in a destruction of traditional temporal rhythms. This is especially ruinous, since the collective concept of an authentic *we* can only emerge from within such rhythms, traditionally sustained from generation to generation. Instead of the real time of the seasons, or shared civic durations, we are now beholden to the imposed "real time" of enmeshed electronic networks, and the kinds of new life patterns they create. In *Acting Out*, Stiegler writes:

> A calendar is a system of synchronization. It defines the rendezvous of the *we*. A rendezvous, in a synchrony of the *we,* makes possible, however, diachronic possibilities. On the other hand, the development of cultural industries leads to a hypersynchronization that eliminates diachronization and paradoxically engenders a hyperdiachronization—that is, a rupture with the symbolic milieu, a decoupling of individual and collective time, a decomposition of the diachronic and the synchronic. The destruction of modes of collective life means that, for example, an adolescent

who returns to the family home at 7 p.m. eats from the fridge, that the father does the same at 8 p.m., and nobody eats with anyone else, the only meeting point being, eventually, the television news. What organizes calendarity is neither local, nor familial, nor national, nor religious—because it is no longer a we—rather, it is the great televisual consumption system. (50)

According to Stiegler, hypersynchronization leads directly to a loss of libido, a forfeit of *joie de vivre*, a disenchantment with world and self. This is because no synchrony of feeling between people can occur in a "symbolic milieu" in which our familiar, habitual chronology has been torn asunder by the rude rhythms and shameless solicitations of new technologies. (Or, to be more precise, the *cynical organization* of new technologies, designed precisely to shatter older modes of being-with, in order to open up new channels and habits of consumption.)

Hypersynchronization is thus the other side of the same coin as hypermodulation, since we would not suffer the former willingly if it were truly a coercive temporality, obliging us all to be in the same virtual space in the same mediated time.[8] We are far more likely to conform to the silent orders of the program industries if we feel we are moving to our own rhythm, oblivious to the higher-order time signature that authorizes these minor and innocuous diversions or divisions. As Mohammed Salemy puts it, "Synchronization regulates all those conflicting network entanglements while we switch from a cat to the revolution. It also replaces the way people organically connect in real-time, so very much like Debord's notion of the spectacle, the disintegrated spectacle of the network replaces the real-time and becomes the omnipresence of a singular temporal logic, despite the contradictoriness of the content of different temporal experiences." Similarly, for Ben Peters, "we could say that synchronization sets the temporal forum, a kind of uniform infrastructure for trivially scalable time measurement, that in turn generates and makes observable and exploitable asynchronous behavior (uncorrelated reading patterns, high-frequency trading, CAP theorem in synchronized databases, etc.)." In other words, hypersynchronization is made up of a thousand tiny asynchronicities. As happens with day trading or credit swaps, the classical clock of the stock market not only allows but facilitates and incorporates more Einsteinian—even quantum—time scales and anomalies. And this itself represents "the industrial exploitation of time" (52), in an ongoing "elimination of general differences" (72). Whether you were born into island time, farm time, jungle time, Bohemian time, factory time, traveler time, or whatever time, social media is calling upon you to abandon such a *specific* relationship to the passing of time and join the masses who all react to the same "events" dictated by the same overarching algorithmic rhythm.

Once again, we have never had more "options" in terms of exposing ourselves to new content, or customizing our various virtual "experiences." There are far more hours of footage uploaded to the Internet in a single day than one human being could possibly watch in an entire lifetime. And yet, as I write, more than two billion people, nearly a third of the world's population, have—voluntarily, I presume—watched Psy's "Gangnam Style" music video. Here, in a nutshell, we see the cozy arrangement between hypersynchronization and hypermodulation. The latter flatters our sense of individuality, by pandering to our own personal preferences and allowing us to create our own "filter bubbles." But the former always wins in the end, as we nevertheless allow the biased topography of the network to usher us toward the latest commercial "event," just as light is sucked inexorably toward a black hole.

For the Italian philosopher Giorgio Agamben, the current world population is nothing less than "the most docile and cowardly social body that has ever existed in human history" (22). This is because of what he sees as our complete capitulation to the forces of libidinal destruction that Stiegler also laments in such exquisite detail. For Agamben—using a different terminology, but coming to an even more pessimistic conclusion—we are being systematically deprived of not only human freedoms, but our own capacity to be subjects of our own lives. Indeed, somewhat ironically, Agamben has a rather Hollywood, *Terminator*-style reading of the situation. While technologies were present at the birth of humanity, what Agamben calls "the apparatus" is depicted as the nemesis of the animal which we essentially are, and which promises so much. And yet this animal chooses to fabricate its own passive mesmerism in ever more portable and ingenious ways, as if we had left the illusional space of Plato's cave only to take little pieces of it with us in our pockets, in the shape of cell phones. (In one extraordinary unphilosophical outburst, Agamben confesses: "I have developed an implacable hatred for this apparatus [the mobile phone], which has made the relationship between people all the more abstract. . . . [Indeed] I found myself more than once wondering how to destroy or deactivate those *telefonini*, as well as how to eliminate or at least to punish and imprison those who do not stop using them" [16].) For Agamben, living beings are in constant, "everyday hand-to-hand struggle with apparatuses" (15), since the latter are "literally anything that has in some way the capacity to capture, orient, determine, intercept, model, control, or secure the gestures, behaviors, opinions, or discourses of living beings" (14).[9] Now that our phones are no longer used for talking but rather as hosts for social media apps, Agamben can only have more reason to curse our misguided enthusiasm in governing ourselves through what Debord called "a generalized autism."

Agamben's system, however, is much too Manichean to really help us navigate the issue, since the only way to escape "the apparatus" is to shed our human skins, and somehow continue in a world now miraculously free of technics. Given that our very souls are forged in techniques of all kinds, this seems closer to wishful messianism than to a political solution. Rather, we need to account for the ways in which infrastructure and ideology mutually reinforce each other, so that we may create strategies to counter their powerful complicity, and so that we may live in something other than what Crary calls "the aftermath of a common life made into the object of technics" (29). Certainly, social media's synchronizing function is so effective that we can only presume Zuckerberg and company are being completely cynical when they celebrate the almost infinite properties of their platforms. After all, they spend billions of dollars to ensure we *don't* use other protocols or divest of social media altogether. And as Crary also warns, "If networks are not in the service of already existing relationships forged out of shared experience and proximity, they will always reproduce and reinforce the separations, the opacity, the dissimulations, and the self-interestedness inherent in their use." Which is to say that "any social turbulence whose primary sources are in the use of social media will inevitably be historically ephemeral and inconsequential" (121). But are these the only two alternatives: the unconscious bondage of social media or the increasingly lonely freedom entailed by logging off? Are there not ways to make use of these new communication tools without succumbing to Silicon Valley's strategic digital interpellation, in which the disingenuous network hails the interactive subject into a self-canceling form of identification?

In a suggestive formula, Paul North writes, "Film teaches us to let go of images" (174). For its part, social media also teaches us to let go of personalized solicitations delivered via image, text, and sound. But it does so *only* in order to make ourselves newly available for the next distracting combination. And the next.

And the next.

2

The Will-to-Synchronize

No question, we are entering uncharted waters when it comes to digital social media. The scale, reach, intensity, and industrial resources involved are all unprecedented, so that we cannot know what the impact may be on our behavior and modes of thinking (indeed, many commentators insist that the very *capacity* for critical thinking, or enabling self-reflection, is being steadily eroded, tweet by tweet). This is a global experiment, occurring in real time: an experiment largely designed by the owners of the means of communication. Some commentators, however, insist that this seemingly sudden explosion of virtual interaction is merely the latest phase of something which is as old as human sociality itself.

Tom Standage, for instance, has made a career of helpfully reminding us that the tendency to fetishize the originality of the present is misguided. To counter this habit, his writing provides precedents, genealogies, and continuities where we presumed there were none. In *The Victorian Internet*, for instance, Standage uncovered cases of flirtations and even marriages occurring "online" in the nineteenth century—through the telegraph, rather than through email or chat programs. This reminds us that there have *always* been different types of "world-wide web," and we would do well to acknowledge this fact, in order to better understand how earlier networks rearranged social structures, cultural arrangements, and psychic habits. In his more recent book, *The Writing on the Wall*, Standage traces the roots of today's social media back to the Roman Empire, when influential citizens relied on a complex constellation of messages, messengers, and media to keep "in the loop" of political affairs, as well as the general goings-on in a thriving network of cities distributed throughout the Mediterranean world. (In this sense, ancient shipping routes were the original pier-to-pier network.) The daily digest of the Senate, known as the *acta diurna populi*

Romani, was copied and recopied many times each day, as news spread through and beyond the *polis*, thanks to the relatively new technologies of wax tablets and writing, as well as the more established technology of a slave class. (The latter, it should be noted, is just as indispensable for today's digital economy—whether the literal slave, mining minerals in Africa or assembling iPhones in China, or the disavowed kind who is paid starvation wages in the overdeveloped nations.)[10] Throughout Rome, the walls of the cities themselves were used as communication interfaces, covered in graffiti dedicated to everything from political campaigns to proto-Yelp reviews of public establishments and services (including, of course, "the world's oldest profession," prostitution). A good deal of such graffiti simply reads as idle Facebook updates or Tweets, as Standage points out:

> At Nuceria, I won 8,552 denarii by gaming—fair play!
> On April 19, I made bread.
> On April 20, I gave a cloak to be washed. On May 7, a headband. On May 8, two tunics.
> . . . .
> Atimetus got me pregnant. (40)

One instance sounds like a surreptitious text message: "The man I am having dinner with is a barbarian."

Standage goes on to credit the next great social media moment to the technological and cultural matrices that allowed Martin Luther to "go viral" (the most crucial element being the invention of the printing press). This in turn anticipates the famous coffeehouses of post-Restoration England, which served as hubs for general gossip, social intrigue, and political plottings. (Standage, following Dunbar, argues in his first chapter that gossip is—and always has been—the essential glue for all human societies, and this is because it serves an evolutionary purpose, as a linguistic extension of the bonding functions of primate grooming.) From this author's perspective, the Internet is merely the latest manifestation of our innate drive for inventing and exploiting "social media." Indeed, this long view of the symbiosis between technology and culture suggests that the Internet may not in fact be the apotheosis of so-called social media (as we assume it to be today). Rather, it may be the current incubation chamber for as-yet unanticipated new types of collective transmission and mediation.

As social creatures of the techno-mammalian class, humans, as a rule, prefer to cluster rather than withdraw. Our default inclination is to extend our senses, via media, to ascertain what else is "going on," beyond those personal horizons, limited by our biological reach. (As McKenzie Wark famously said, "We no longer have roots, we have aerials.") We are curious animals . . . in both senses. Even when we can curate our own perfect media environment, we tend to feel isolated or restless if we are too long deprived of receiving real-time signals from our scattered neighbors. Those readers old enough to remember what it was like to live before the Internet will recall the strange phenomenon where the general noosphere seduced us by its sheer beckoning presence. Thus, we would find ourselves listening to terrible songs or talk shows on the radio in the car rather than listening to our perfectly sequenced mixtape or intriguing audiobook. Or we would end up flicking from channel to channel on the TV, preferring this cathodic wasteland to the stack of quality VHS videos that sat neglected in the corner of the living room. Such perverse behavior exhibits a profound and tenacious *will-to-synchronize*. Indeed, this is the source and continuing energy supply for everything we call "media" (or what Stiegler calls, following Derrida, our "grammaticization"). This crucial characteristic shapes the general desire to connect with the signals and traces of other monads, no matter how tedious or embarrassing these signals and traces may be. (Just take a look at the top ten movies, TV shows, and albums right now, for ample evidence of this claim.)

Broadly speaking, this will-to-synchronize occurs on at least five interlocking planes: the evolutionary (biological), the metaphysical (social-spiritual), the affective (phenomenological), the historical (technical, biopolitical), and the post-historical (libidinal-ecological). While we can find any of these planes comprising the architecture of any moment in the history of hominization, they are also—by virtue of ratios and sedimentations—periodic or epochal layers. So to say, the first plane provides the foundation for the subsequent ones, giving them all a chronological aspect. In terms of the first plane, our will-to-synchronize exhibits itself in order to reproduce and continue the species (driven by our DNA, or "the selfish gene"). Here we find lust and attraction, and all those things we do in an ongoing attempt to gratify bodily appetites (and to have better odds of survival, according to the law of safety in numbers). On the second plane, we seek to *make sense* of these primal urges, beyond mere assembly for its own sake, and the organic imperative to persist and procreate. On this plane we synchronize our activities with the seasons, the gods, the cosmos—and we look for signs that help us orient ourselves in this uncanny valley known as existence. Here we try to work together within a single, overarching raison d'être: whether this be called "religion" or "art" (both connected to aesthetics, as is the first plane, in fact, when it comes to the dance between beauty and seduction). The third plane—co-terminous with the second—is where we try to make further sense of these collective signals for our own individual context: where a self-reflexive subject navigates the blessings and terrors of being one solitary will among many others (usually coming into conflict with our own). On this plane, however, cultural rituals reinforce the collectivity over the self, partly as a way of keeping a homeo-static state between human atoms that threaten to go rogue. And this occurs within the frame of a greater social project which we are obliged to fit in to. The fourth plane is where we start to recognize and reflect on patterns amongst our collective endeavors, and the narratives we put upon them: where we have been, and where we think we are going (and/or *should* go). Here we are swept up in a larger trajectory and momentum. And this is where we elaborate and refine discussions of conduct and ethics, first encountered on the religious plane, but now no longer conceived as moral prescriptions from *beyond*. Rather, these new imperatives emerge from within the greater human project, unmoored from celestial designs. This is where we become our own "prosthetic gods," using rapidly evolving technologies to manage and administer the new understanding of—and relation to—*life* (and, thus, death). Political programs are paramount here, determined on macroeconomic principles. We ask ourselves, "What is to be done?" (now that, as a species, we are no longer told what to do by invisible agents). And finally, the fifth plane is in fact more of a precipice, and one we are all teetering on at present. Here we find a pervasive bewilderment and insecurity, exacerbated by loss of shared chronology, direction, or purpose. (What Stiegler calls "disorientation," due to a forfeiture of access to *cardinality* and *calendrical-ity*: the once stable parameters of space and time.) The environment is thus revealed to us as "eco-logical" at the same moment that it is lost to us as a *place* of unthinking habitation. And in the same stroke, "nature" is revealed to us as a retrospective *space* of romantic-phantasmatic projection.

The kind of will-to-synchronize I have been describing in our own lives—the millennial kind, emerging in the late twentieth century, and extending into today—is one deeply colored by the experience of alienation. (Or, rather, it is colored by the *anti*-experience of alienation, since according to the critical theorists we rarely, if ever, encounter any experience worth having.) This is why we hope the remote control, or the smart-phone, will reveal to us the semi-magical "lives of others," which for some reason, unconnected to logic or experience (but heavily suggested by the Spectacle), promises something *more* than what we ourselves have (or *feel* we have). Now that pre-vious "organic" modes of community have been shattered by the forces of capitalist modernization, and we are thrown into a sea of confused human-ity, we feel, paradoxically, cut off from our fellow man and woman. ("Water water everywhere /

Nor any drop to drink.") Gossip now comes to us not so much from the neighbor, relation, or co-worker, but the TV show, the radio broadcast, or the website newsfeed. Thus, we postmodern folk are haunted by a will-to-synchronize, left bereft in a temporal landscape littered with the debris of previous forms of being-together (what Heidegger called *Mitsein*, or "with-being").

Certainly, this is a crude "grand narrative"—the kind that Jean-François Lyotard warned us against taking too seriously. And yet few would dispute the general thrust, and import, of smaller, relatively coherent social groups being violently subsumed into much larger ones through colonization, urbanization, industrialization, globalization, and so forth. While every generation in the Western hemisphere, since the invention of writing—or even the invention of language—may have feared that it had been left to pick up the pieces of a formerly unified Arcadia, we know today that we are producing more and more toxic and tangible fragments of betrayed human solidarity and "lived experience." Every piece of trash washing back up on the seashore, every image lapping at our tired retinas, bears witness to the shattered ideal of our once promising species-being. Which only makes us more desperate to distract ourselves from our own existential belatedness and perplexity, while holding out hope that we will soon find "the one" to make this ordeal seem somehow "worth it"— or, at the very least, make some kind of sense. (And "the one" here need not be a messianic lover, but could equally be a teacher, a guru, a health coach, a life coach, a yoga teacher, or a suburban spirit guide.)

Letters, telegrams, telephones, "the talkies," newspapers, ham radios, car radios, television . . . and of course social media: all of these have helped us at least *try* to put our lonely souls in sync with others, and find an acceptable likeness of what Georges Bataille described as existential "continuity." Such media, whether analog or digital, aid us in our attempts to receive a continuous feed from what we might call "the banal beyond": the virtual space *somewhere out there*, where significant decisions are made, where people know things you do not, where life is lived *as it should be*. (Baudrillard: "Porno says: somewhere there is true sex, since I am its caricature" [*Revenge* 152].) Hence the power of Hollywood, which promises to teach us how to desire and how to live (which is essentially the same thing). Somewhere, in our own minds, there is a picture of a functioning society in which we fit, but we feel like a jig-saw piece that has been abandoned in a basement. And the box—which boasted the completed image—has also gone missing; so we don't have a map to help us put everything together again. And *this* is what propels our appetite for distraction. Every status update, every tweet, every post, every tumbl, every selfie promises to add up to that lost picture and reflection of premodern society that Durkheim described in such detail. Instead, each digital tid-bit threatens to obscure the image further, as the shiny surface loses its power to reveal anything other than our own *personal* reflections. We thus lose any sense of a "we" at all.

This is the danger, in any case. But we must not get too caught up in nostalgic rhetoric, since this is as likely to foreclose or obscure possible exit strategies as the new technologies we find so easy to demonize (even as we rely on them for almost everything besides breathing). In other words, we should not lose sight of the many enabling and encouraging uses and potentials of social media (as strange as this may sound, after the common doomsday scenario sketched above). Indeed, some critics play the devil's advocate with such enthusiasm that they even argue that what appears to be distraction, to us analog humans, is in fact the birth of a new, superior digital-species, capable of dexterous multitasking and mental parallel processing.[11] The next super-human is nigh, ushering in the Singularity. The question remains, however, to what degree this is an evolutionary shift shaped by the capitalist requirement to adapt to the machine, rather than by our own freedom and agency. At any rate, the chorus of voices condemning the global addiction to social media all too often rings hollow, especially when we take Standage's long view into account, and see such technologies, and their uses, as simply (and not so simply) the latest iteration of cultural communication, albeit one uniquely vulnerable to being observed and controlled.

We certainly find ourselves interacting online for a constellation of different reasons. Some seek company, others specific information. Some crave distractions, while others scan the wires with the focused intensity of a laser beam. We can find instructions, advice, suggestions, recommendations; often volunteered out of the goodness of someone's own heart, and a general sense of helpfulness toward others. The Facebook newsfeed is often treated like the town square, town hall, and town crier, all at once. Moreover, it can function as virtual school, tavern, press, library, salon, catwalk, gallery, market, movie palace, agony aunt, and matchmaker. We can listen to someone speaking on their soapbox and respond in kind. Or we can witness an exchange inconspicuously, like someone in sunglasses in the corner of a café—watching, speculating, judging. We can ask for assistance, we can conduct informal polls, we can savor the sweetness of the honeyed hive-mind when it responds positively to our questions (or curse it when it greets our earnest question with silence or sarcasm). We can fish for compliments or enjoy giving them to others. We can humblebrag and self-promote. We can commiserate, congratulate, and congregate. Certainly in my own case, I use various social media feeds as my primary daily interface with the wider world, and would feel lost without it. (Most of us now know the feeling of near-physical panic when the Internet goes down, and we are literally left to our own—unconnected—devices. Increasingly, however, the world spares us such anxious moments by providing a second electronic umbilical cord, thanks to smartphones and cell towers.)

The gift of social media is indeed the gift of remote and imperfect (or asymptotic) mass-synchronization. I find here, literally on the same (web)page, a cornucopia of links, information, and exchanges—certainly more than I can really register or digest. This kind of nodal centralization means that I can find travel tips, upcoming conferences, new music, film recommendations, political commentary, social justice activism, and tempting recipes, all in one place. And many of these are likely to resonate with me, since they are provided by friends, and friends of friends. (If they don't resonate with me, then I can hide or unfriend them.)[12] Beyond this, the Kevin Bacon principle means that I can sense waves of potential relationships lapping at my door. Indeed, one positive aspect of online spaces like Facebook is that they provide a rare intergenerational gathering space, where people of different vintages can share experiences and interests in an ongoing game of "show and tell." While such fleeting glimpses and (largely unclicked) links may not qualify as Stiegler's much-needed "long loops"—or pedagogic chains—these scrolling *short* loops at least have the virtue of opening windows onto worlds that were previously shut fast between generations that would mostly interact in only formal or familial circumstances. (Then again, we are often told that younger people only join and suffer Facebook for coercive family reasons, and hardly spend any time there at all, preferring chat programs and more image-based platforms, like Instagram and Tumblr.)

In her short meditation on the specific affective exchanges of Facebook, the celebrated cultural critic Lauren Berlant begins with an anecdote:

> Today I introduced Facebook to someone older than me and had a long conversation about what the point of networking amongst "friends" is. The person was so skeptical because to her stranger and distance-shaped intimacies are diminished forms of real intimacy. To her, real intimacy is a relation that requires the fortitude and porousness of a serious, emotionally-laden, accretion of mutual experience. Her intimacies are spaces of permission not only for recognition but for the right to be seriously inconvenient, to demand, and to need. It presumes face to faceness, but even more profoundly, flesh to

fleshness. But on Facebook one can always skim, or not log in.[13]

Berlant's own perspective, however, is that social media allows a more ambiguous space: neither inherently lamentable nor worthy of celebration, but allowing different degrees of attention, alternative "investment" strategies, and less taxing forms of exchange than those we encounter offline. For her, "the stretched-out intimacies" of digital communication matter precisely *because* they are "more shaped by the phantasmatic dimension of recognition and reciprocity." When online, "it is easier to hide inattention, disagreement, disparity, aversion." Thus, there is less likely to be "collateral damage" in "mediated or stranger intimacies." In Berlant's view, social media allows us to communicate in less demanding ways—more playful and glancing—because they are somehow "atmospheric." Interactions in this register thus have an almost climatic dimension. The micro-thoughts and semiotic gestures of other, unseen, people waft in like fog, breezes, or spells of sunshine, only to quickly evaporate or condense into something else. (Indeed, one of the most popular pastimes online is "venting"—a term with linguistic roots in the Latin word for *wind*.) And these signals arrive unanchored by the heaviness of another's presence; by the facticity of another flesh-and-blood person, which in its somatic assertions is incapable of *not* making mute bodily demands on one's emotional resources.

For some, especially those who found themselves in adulthood before the turn of the millennium, this evacuation of the actual *is* the main problem with social media. To many in this group, it seems like an evasion or abdication of responsibility to alterity, in all its brute and sensuous immediacy. To others (and we should not be too dogmatic about age or generations, since there are a great deal of zealous "silver surfers," just as there are plenty of teenage techno-skeptics), interaction via the network is not a *replacement* for "real" communication, but a somewhat freeing alternative space: a valuable adjunct to the face to face, precisely in its superficial supplementarity. Interestingly, Berlant incorporates the notion of synchronization into her poetics of social media, referencing its novel strategies and capacities for "coordinating lives." Within the wider contemporary (and technical) project of "synchronizing being," Facebook rather ironically removes the face of the other and replaces it with a more telegraphic presence, with a lighter touch. This affords a different type of synchrony to embodied interactions: one that encourages "all kinds of emotional dependency and sustenance [that] can flourish amongst people who only meet each other at one or a few points on the grid of the field of their life." This "light impact" mode of intersection—constituted by a great deal of "echoing and noodling"—renders reciprocity easy, promiscuous, spontaneous. "It's not in the idiom of the great encounter or the great passion," Berlant writes; "it's the lightness and play of the poke. There's always a potential but not a demand for more."[14]

And yet the will-to-sync is thwarted from many angles and on many occasions. The more we try to synchronize, the more dissonance enters the frame. We may want to talk about movies but find we have disturbingly different tastes to our interlocutors. We may want to talk about the weather, but we live in different hemispheres. At every point that we are drawn toward an ideal(ized) merger with an abstract companion, the stubborn or petty concrete other blocks our path. Yet our devices promise to give us access to the Big Other, simply by virtue of its networked status and constantly "refreshing" character. The portable device is a portal to elsewhere, which, by the deferred logic of greener grass, is better than wherever the user finds themselves. (Indeed, smartphones tempt us to speculate that Lacan's *objet petit a* has finally been identified, captured, tamed—as if the inherently virtual had magically crystallized into an object. Or, rather, an encased vector to our endlessly deferred desires.)[15]

Think also of all those disconcerting temporal stutters, delays, and drop-outs that occur when we try to "reach out and touch someone." A friend (or potential friend) may be texting on a train that suddenly rushes into a tunnel, and we lose the connection. Or we might assume we're in the middle of a chat, while our interlocutor suddenly treats the conversation like email, to be picked up later, leaving us to wonder unhappily if we've offended. Or our chat box may be trumped by someone more interesting or desirable popping up on the other's screen, leaving us in the lurch. ("Hello. Are you still there?") The mutual temporality we thought we were sharing is shown to be partial, provisional, easily abandoned, without the usual gestures to soften the blow of social abandonment or neglect. Worse still, we may never really know if we're in the midst of a conversation or not, making the threads more difficult to pick up at a later date. As a result, interaction online can often feel warped and treacherous; especially for those who have internalized the more analog protocols and niceties of interpersonal discourse. We find ourselves obliged to communicate within a new kind of space-time *dis*continuum. (And here we might be cavalier enough to fuse a caricature of Freud with a sketch of Heidegger, and claim that social media encourages an unsettling sense of *fort-da(sein)*—of being *here* and *there* at the same time . . . which is tantamount to being nowhere in particular. We are thus un-homed by a scrambled sense of our own *adeixis*, as well as that of others.)[16]

For Berlant, however, the temporality of social media is primarily defined not by these kinds of dropped connections, but by the ways in which these can be swiftly picked up by others, in what she calls the "episodic now." Facebook in particular, by this account, concerns itself with "calibrating the difficulty of knowing the importance of the ordinary event." In other words, "people are trying there to eventalize the mood, the inclination, the thing that just happened—the episodic nature of existence." Whatever publicity stunt or random viral content is clamoring to "break the Internet" at any given time strives—or threatens—to become an event. These kinds of events, however, arrive (mercifully) "without the drama of a disturbance."

For an earlier critic of quotidian affect, Henri Lefebvre, everyday life is "unmediated" (651). While his later writings (from the 1980s) began to grapple presciently with the coming cybernetic revolution, busily dismantling any distinction between the immediate and machinically chaperoned, Lefebvre could not envision the amniotic digital world we have created for ourselves. Thus, his working principle of the everyday was based on a kind of *lived* reality, no matter how annexed or alienated by the complicity between capital and advanced technics. This is meat-based Marxism. But where Berlant finds a kind of relief, or space of play, amidst the tidal currents of pseudo-events online—events which barely bother to clear their throat before departing—Lefebvre sees grounds for hope in humanity's future within "the moment." Lefebvre has a very specific and sophisticated "theory of moments" which plucks them from the prosaic flow of everyday life, without fully transcending it. Less than an event, yet more than a mere given situation, this definition of the moment is designed to identify and promote "the seeds of every possibility."

"Through all the changes," Lefebvre writes, "'something' remains. We would say that 'something' is the *moment*" (636). That is, "'something'—which is certainly not a thing—is encountered once again. Both an illusion and a reality, *lived time* appears once more through all the veils and distances. It vanishes, and at the same time it makes itself known" (636, emphasis added). Among such moments, "we may include love, play, rest, knowledge, etc." Sounding a lot like Alain Badiou at times, albeit on a humbler register, Lefebvre states that the moment "*is constituted by a choice which singles it out and separates it from a muddle or a confusion, i.e., from an initial ambiguity.*" As such, it is "relatively durable" and "stands out from the continuum of transitories within the amorphous realm of the psyche. It wants to endure. It cannot endure (at least, not for very long). Yet this inner contradiction gives it its intensity" (639).

Whether the moment designates a torrid love affair, a stimulating game, a risky wager, the dogged pursuit of solving a problem, an urgent project, or a successful attempt to extricate oneself from the tendrils of work, Lefebvre's *moment* emerges out of the humdrum routine of existence in order to better illuminate its contours and limitations. "The moment is born of the everyday and within the everyday," he explains further. "From here it draws its nourishment and its substance; and this is the only way it can deny the everyday. It is in the everyday that a possibility becomes apparent (be it play, work or love, etc.) in all its brute spontaneity and ambiguity" (645).[17] Thus, Lefebvre calls the moment "*the attempt to achieve the total realization of a possibility*"—an attempt doomed to failure, as that is the nature of time ("This too shall pass.") Thus, the mundane routines we endure are revealed as secretly tragic. Indeed, there is some salvation in that, by virtue of realizing that (real) moments pulse beneath the mere metronomic monotony of our days. "It is a festival, it is a marvel, but it is not a miracle." Which *is* in fact the miracle: that something meaningful is immanent to our (usually) forsaken situation.

What does this all have to do with social media?

The connection is uncovered when we update Lefebvre's notion of "unmediated lived reality" into today's information networks, where much of our everyday life is now conducted. Certainly, as already signaled, Lefebvre was not unaware of the growing power of technocratic industries and ideologies during the great neoliberal counter-reformation of the 1980s, when "the optimistic prophecies of technicians and official circles have invaded the media" (808). What he called "the formalization of daily life" had already severed the all-important membrane between the *concrete* (human) experience and the *abstract* (ideal), collapsing them together into a monstrous hybrid, and robbing the power that each had when standing on its own two feet. People start to lose their substance, as they are decanted into abstract equations, supposedly created for their benefit but which instead quantify them into commodified units, ready for easy deployment. ("All that is solid melts into air.")

Sounding remarkably like Stiegler (whom he undoubtedly influenced), Lefebvre writes:

The creative capacity of communication and information is slowly but surely exhausted.

With each new means of communication and information—for example, electricity (the "electricity fairy!," "electrification plus soviets!"), and then the telephone, radio, television—people anticipate miracles: the transfiguration of daily life. As if it could come from a means or medium. These means or media can only transmit what existed prior to the mediating operation, or what occurs outside it. Today, communication *reflects*—nothing more, nothing less. What was the result of the multiplication of these means in ever more complex forms? Rather than a metamorphosis of daily life, what occurred was, on the contrary, the installation of daily life as such, determined, isolated, and then programmed. There ensued a privatization of the public and a publicizing of the private, in a constant exchange that mixes them without uniting them and separates them without discriminating between them; and this is still going on. (815)

Such new arrangements risk "the destruction of meaning by signs" (Baudrillard's arch-theme, of course). Moreover, "the increasing intensity of communications harbours the reinforcement of daily life, its consolidation and confinement."

One of the greatest dangers Lefebvre warns against is the extinction of spaces reserved for critical thought, unhobbled by positivist exigencies. As if foreseeing the corporate enthusiasm for Massive Open Online Courses (or MOOCs), Lefebvre writes (in a crucial paragraph, worth quoting in full):

Not only does information ideology not present itself as ideology, but it proposes either to put an end to ideologies or to transfer the ideological function to information apparatuses, including the production and diffusion of positive knowledge, which was formerly the prerogative of schools and universities. The *reduction of positive knowledge to information* would have consequences: the end of critical and conceptual thinking, and hence the end of all thinking, or its departure to take refuge in illegality and violence. All the more so given that information apparatuses are in great danger of being administratively and institutionally controlled either by the national state, or by transnational forces which would use this supplementary means to consolidate their order. Not only would positive knowledge be reduced to recorded and memorized facts,[18] but everything concerning the political and politics would go through the channels of official information. This would create the greatest difficulties for any action independent of established power, and possibly result in the disappearance of all counter-power. (819, emphasis added)

This is a different kind of will-to-synchronization that we have been considering thus far, although they are intimately connected (sadly, increasingly so). In *this* case, the will comes from above, from the social architects, and harnesses the will of the masses in bad faith, and for its own purposes. "Information," Lefebvre writes, "together with its extensions, would lead by the shortest route to a fully planned society, in which the centre would constantly receive messages from each base cell, with the result that culture and information, positively identified, possessing the same structure, would render each individual fully conscious" (820). In such a schema we see the centralized rhizome of the Internet (or Google, or the NSA), *avant la lettre*. Describing the as-yet fledgling Silicon Valley with great foresight, Lefebvre makes reference to "the myth of an electronic Agora," which is little more than a "scientistic mythology." Moreover, the proto-Zuckerberg ideologues that live there "do not think that they are interpreting the techniques, but that they are estimating them objectively. They refuse to concede that they are presenting, or representing, a tendentious political project" (821). A dangerous state of affairs indeed, when those in control of the planetary communications infrastructure consider it to be ideologically neutral, and thus forging its own direction and valences.

Finally, Lefebvre finishes his massive, three-volume study of everyday life with a nightmarish vision that could be straight out of the pages of the Gothic novel that he warned us against writing (quoted as the epigraph of this book), when discussing information technologies. Anticipating the current age of Facebook, he writes:

Computerized daily life risks assuming a form that certain ideologues find interesting and seductive: the individual atom or family molecule inside a bubble where the messages sent and received intersect. Users, who have lost the dignity of citizens now that they figure socially only as parties to services, would thus lose the social itself, and sociability. This would no longer be the existential isolation of the old individualism, but a solitude all the more profound for being overwhelmed by messages. (823)

We can only speculate whether Lefebvre would have continued to hold out hope for the revolutionary potential of "moments" in an age when it could be argued that the majority of everyday life is conducted online. One suspects that he would consider "lived reality" to be a rapidly dwindling resource, exponentially evaporating, now that it has been severed from its source of "unmediated" interpersonal contact. The social has migrated into machinic mediation itself, and thus perhaps lost even the potentially recreative residues of its alienated sociality. Today we find ourselves merely "bombarded by a hubbub."

Perhaps haunted by premonitions of iChats, conducted via cutesy speech bubbles, Lefebvre (823) ends his tome on a chilling note: "People talk about a new society. Would it not be more accurate to fear a new state, founded on the political use of information, ruling over a population enclosed in bubbles it has inflated, and in such a way that each mouth believes its bubble comes out of it?"

3

Slaves to the Algorithm

What we see in our social media feeds is almost always carefully calibrated to keep stimulating our general appetite for distraction. Beyond the solicitous content perfected by sites like Buzzfeed—which specialize in "click bait" phrases and images that forever promise more than they deliver ("You won't BELIEVE what happens next!")—there are the algorithms that determine which posts we see and which we do not. Facebook notoriously curates the user's content for them while allowing only a modicum of configurability within the larger parameters of the platform. But only a minority of users realize just how tailored their experience is (with a heavy bias toward targeted advertising, of course). In the natural world, the spider configures its web to the precise specifics of the fly. Silicon Valley does the same with us, spinning its "sticky" offerings to our exhaustively researched demographic measurements.

When our information architecture is built on such shifting sands, it is likely to turn us all into paranoiacs ("no one likes me anymore"), while also giving those who disappoint us—by not "liking" a post, for instance—an unverifiable "out." (Which only leads to further paranoia.) Did so-and-so really not see my post? Or are they using the algorithm as an alibi to ignore my updates? Such is the kind of second-guessing that Facebook in particular produces in us. (That is, when we aren't being explicitly slighted by the inevitable disconnect between our own desires, and the busyness or indifference of others.) No wonder, then, that we encounter a steady stream of articles confirming what we already know: the more we "share" online, the more our mood is negatively affected, as we feel we don't get anything of equal value in return.[19] A tiny, pixelated icon of a "thumbs-up" does not suffice as social registration of the good faith and vulnerable courage involved when sharing anxieties, hopes, or meaningful moments. To say nothing of the fear that we might be posting a link or story that has been deemed "so five minutes ago" by the rest of the hive-mind. (One of many unwritten online *faux pas*.) Our personal stock can plummet if we unknowingly link to a story or video two months after everyone else. Hence the pressure to "keep our eyes on the feed," in case we miss a major meme, and thus a virtual "water cooler" micro-event.

Indeed, shifts in Facebook's algorithm are like shifts in the winds or the waxing and waning of the moon. Suddenly someone who hasn't liked any of your posts for a long time likes three of them in a row, while a serial liker suddenly neglects your witticisms or timely links. (Of course, *all* your friends would like *all* your posts, if only it weren't for Zuckerberg's digital blinkers popping up and down.) At such moments, we realize that we are interfacing with the wider electronic world in a kind of Matrix-like digital structure that can be moved about at will from above, as if a building could have its rooms suddenly rearranged, to enable new neighbors or vistas. No doubt, this capacity—to code and recode specific semiotic environments in order to best capture the user's attention—is an important aspect of Stiegler's concept of *hypersynchronization*. And yet, as we have already established several times, we are also being hyper*modulated*.

Take, for instance, Facebook's admission that it decided to tinker with specific users' feeds—unbeknownst to them—as part of an experiment to try to determine whether "emotional states can be transferred to others via emotional contagion, leading people to experience the same emotions without their awareness."[20] The initial findings of this ethically dubious piece of research, conducted by Adam Kramer, Jamie Guillory, and Jeffrey Hancock, suggested that "longer-lasting moods (e.g., depression, happiness) can be transferred through networks, although the results are controversial." In the authors' own words:

> We test[ed] whether emotional contagion occurs outside of in-person interaction between individuals by reducing the amount of emotional content in the [Facebook] News Feed. When positive expressions were reduced, people produced fewer positive posts and more negative posts; when negative expressions were reduced, the opposite pattern occurred. These results indicate that emotions

expressed by others on Facebook influence our own emotions, constituting experimental evidence for massive-scale contagion via social networks. This work also suggests that, in contrast to prevailing assumptions, in-person interaction and nonverbal cues are not strictly necessary for emotional contagion, and that the observation of others' positive experiences constitutes a positive experience for people.[21]

When this study was announced, there was a flurry of articles in (what remains of) the mainstream press, accusing Zuckerberg and his operation of deliberately manipulating people's moods and minds without considering the possible dangerous consequences (in more extreme cases, possible suicide or murder—especially if the user is already unstable, and provoked by a steady stream of dark information). For while "the media" has been deliberately playing with our emotions for decades (some would say centuries), Facebook was accused of performing such experiments in "emotional engineering" on an unprecedented scale, and with cutting-edge tools. As Laurie Penny wrote in the *New Statesman*, "Nobody has ever had this sort of power before.

No dictator in their wildest dreams has been able to subtly manipulate the daily emotions of more than a billion humans so effectively. . . . What the company does now will influence how the corporate powers of the future understand and monetize human emotion."[22] This territory gets even murkier when we recall that in 2010 Facebook indulged in another experiment, this time deploying "get out and vote" banners connected to users' friends in the United States, which apparently resulted in an increase of 340,000 votes across the country. And while people don't tend to get mad about a bump in democratic participation, this statistical spike should give us pause, considering the potential such "experiments" represent in terms of influencing voting behavior in general (no matter the direction).[23]

The stakes were raised even higher when OK Cupid subsequently admitted that they had deliberately sent a certain subset of their lonely-hearts user base on "bad dates" in order to conduct some experiments of their own: part of a wider attempt to correlate data-determined incompatibility and emotional responses.[24] (OK Cupid's public "trends" page, it must be said,

makes fascinating reading: crunching the numbers between things like stated attraction levels
across racial, economic, and/or gender identity
markers.)[25] More troubling than a corporation
consciously playing incompetent matchmaker,
and perhaps putting already emotionally vulnerable people at risk from an increased likelihood
of rejection, were the subsequent apologetics for
such conduct by a certain cross-section of the general public. At the time this scandal was exposed,
the two dominant responses, represented via
social media, seemed to be a sense of outrage
and betrayal that a company would do such a
thing to "us," the loyal users, and a shoulder-
shrugging sense of amusement at the very idea of
thousands of (probable) bad dates orchestrated
by a mischievous algorithm.[26] After all, the latter
group told us, *that's the deal.* We use social media
platforms to communicate in new, fun, and con-
venient ways—for free. And in return we sign the
absurdly detailed legal agreements that reserve the
right of the company to vacuum up our personal
information and use it for their own purposes.
This latter group seems cynically unfazed by the
Internet dictum, "If the service is free, then you
are the product," since they consider it a fair quid

pro quo. But things get further into the gray zone when companies start actively experimenting on their users, manipulating certain scenarios and results in order to make them repeatable and veri-fiable. The old dream of controlling the *demos* from above or afar—as if the people are nothing more than sound waves, being manipulated by a giant mixing desk—finally moves from being a hubristic dream to a true possibility. So-called "big data" occurs on a scale too large to account for actual individual lives; they are of no impor-tance. The only thing that registers is the curve, the sine wave, the overlapping data points.[27]

Indeed, we moderns are surprisingly oblig-ing in our willingness to become guinea pigs for such endeavors. Take the current Fitbit craze, for example. With this so-called smart bracelet, we willingly place a tracking device on our wrist with many of the same functions as those affixed to the ankles of convicted felons, to ensure they do not leave a restricted area. But because the Fitbit has been "gamified"—because we can compete with friends for the most steps in a day, meas-uring our progress on a shared app page—we find it more fun than disturbing, more an oppor-tunity to remotely keep up with others than a mode of surveillance that erodes a century or so of hard-won civil liberties. ("This life may be monitored or recorded for training and quality control purposes.")[28] But even if we limit our digital gadgets to smartphones, we still have a GPS-tracking device in our pockets, leaving an electronic record wherever we go, glittering silver through Google's Street View like a cybersnail trail. (Which in itself answers the implied question in the subtitle of this book: who is *really* paying attention to social media? The police.[29] The Pentagon.[30] The NSA.[31] The CIA.[32])

Thus the traditional dystopian scenario of the nineteenth and twentieth centuries changes in the age of social media, no longer a bleak, black-and-white world of uniform movement and homogeneous expression, but a colorful, "fun," personalized experience, in which we all dance to our own drum. (On the condition that we listen to this rhythm through Apple's iPod earbuds or Dr. Dre's branded "Beats" headphones.) We are invited to blaze our own pathway through the world, so long as we leave our legible (and leverageable) data shadow in our wake. Social media allows, even encourages, self-tailored lines of flight; all the better to *re*territorialize these into a continuous coding operation that can then anticipate, and incorporate, such options into the database. This is the insight that Roland Barthes gave us, long before the Internet was part of the popular imaginary. "Before anything else," Barthes writes, "the first thing that power imposes is a rhythm (to everything: a rhythm of life, of time, of thought, of speech)" (35). Those who are *subjected* to power—the populace in general—are obliged to synchronize themselves to this rhythm, or risk being synchronized from above. We fall into the rhythm of work, and the sub-rhythms and counter-punctual beats that the world of labor creates for us (rhythms of thinking, speaking, acting, eating, moving . . . being). In contrast to the disciplinary, hegemonic rhythm of society, Barthes posits "idiorhythmy"—"where each subject lives according to his own rhythm" (6).[33]

Idiorhythmy is a rare thing, tolerated only in specific sites and moments in history (or in literature), usually of only a few dozen souls (such as monks at Mt. Athos, or communes of various kinds, both real and imaginary).[34] For Barthes, "the demand for idiorhythmy is always made in opposition to power" (35). Were he alive today, we can speculate that Barthes would not have considered our personalized, "freelance" schedules as true idiorhythmy, because—if we zoom out into long shot—the different speeds and circuits have been anticipated for us by the various authorized networks we move about within. No matter if we sleep late, play the drums all afternoon, and then take a conference call with Shanghai in the evening. As long as there is a deadline, we adapt to the musical timesheet of that dominant rhythm. As long as social media is obliging us to "keep up with the Kardashians" (or the Trumps or the Putins), our own would-be idiorhythmy is surreptitiously absorbed into the highly synchronized tempos of the program industries.

Given the different platforms that constitute "social media," it is difficult to generalize about their dominant forms of temporality. Information cycles can turn faster or slower, depending on how many friends, contacts, or co-users you or the sub-system has. Webcams, for instance, provide a very different aperture onto things from the fast editing of action movies or music videos, while Reality TV—itself now enfolded by the sensitive tentacles of social media—combines these very different speeds into its format. We might also consider national attempts to desynchronize themselves from the pace of the wider world, as Norway has recently been consciously doing with its "Slow TV" moment, featuring shows dedicated to single shots of a train journey, a fireplace burning, birds building nests, or even a woman knitting, all for several hours at a time. (Indeed, the remarkably high ratings for these meditative programs gives hope for the future— at least in Scandinavia.) But as a rule, things rise to the surface and then disappear back down into obscurity, in the blink of an eye. Andy Warhol's prophecy of accelerated micro-fame has come true. Paradoxically, this general breathlessness of information exchange afflicts techno-abstainers and late adopters, even more than those who comfortably inhabit the digital ecosystem; at least, so argues Rob Horning, one of our most acute observers of social media. "Facebook is possibly more in the foreground for those who don't use it than for those who have accepted it as social infrastructure," he writes. "You have to expend more effort not knowing a meme than letting it pass through you." The danger for those who try to resist the new digital idiocy is falling "out of sync with the flow of life."[35] (And I use "idiocy" here in both senses, Barthes's and the pejorative.)[36] Thus, Horning adds, "the inescapable reciprocity of social relations comes into much sharper relief when you stop using social media, which thrive on the basis of the control over reciprocity they try to provide. They give a crypto-dashboard to social life, making it seem like a personal consumption experience, but that is always an illusion, always scattered by the anxiety of waiting, watching for responses, and by the whiplash alternation between omnipotence and vulnerability."

In other words, the evolving infrastructures of social media pull us in two different directions. On the one hand, we are being increasingly herded toward the same stories, the same sites, the same viral pseudo-events, thanks to protocols like hashtags and other trending signals. On the other hand, our digital diet has lost its daily punctuation, thanks to the recent vast increase in "time-shifted" consumption. (Indeed, the very phrase *time-shift* is transitional, marking a new media paradigm which only makes sense in relation to more established modes of viewership—which is why it will no doubt fall out of the lexicon soon, when people have forgotten that we once all watched the same thing at the same time.) Not so long ago, families and friends gathered around the same broadcasts: whether it be FDR on the radio or the moonwalk on the TV. Today, the five-member family is more likely to be absorbed in five different screens, watching—or interacting with—five different virtual spaces. From this perspective, social media in fact "disrupts" the general *synchronization* afforded by broadcast media, in contrast to Stiegler's account. Now we are scooped up by individual butterfly nets, rather than the one big rat trap of TV. Here, however, the dialectic reappears (and this is where the "hyper" comes from in Stiegler's term). While we may seem to all be distracted by different shows, sites, programs, and devices, this is in fact a mirage, since we are all plugged into the same circuits, the same logic, the same imperatives, and the same ideological apparatuses. The first level fracturing reveals itself, at a deeper level, to be about hypersynchronizing us back into the same grid (no matter where our own consumer presence shows up on the various sectors of this grid). We can watch all the most popular shows whenever we want to now, not when the network tells us to. And yet, we are still expected, even *obliged*, to watch them. Otherwise, what will we have to talk about when we meet our friends in real life next?

Indeed, the tension between focusing and dispersal—synchronizing and modulating— is embedded in the ubiquitous phrase "spoiler alert." This term emerges in our language at the precise moment when no one can be sure to be watching the same thing at the same time, as used to happen with, say, the *M*A*S*H* finale. But the assumption is that we will "catch up" at some point, even if we miss a show being served hot to the populace for the first time, like televisual pizza, straight out of the oven. It bears repeating (or reheating). Entertainment media thus becomes spatial, rather than temporal: a dynamic form of architecture that we climb around like a monkey puzzle tree, discovering "new" stories from different eras, no longer approaching them with a sense of history or chronology. The Netflix browser becomes a rummage sale where we might find Tarkovsky's *Solaris* hidden underneath a pile of Adam Sandler flicks. Thus, we interact in a new Nowhen, in which we feel entitled to angrily say, "Spoiler alert!" when our interlocutor is discussing anything from *Breaking Bad* to *Beowulf*.

The overall effect of this kind of torsion between the syncing up of human interests and behaviors and the inevitable differences these encounter is like those videos that digital artists now make, overlaying every episode of *Friends*, or those meta-images comprising every cover of *Vogue* all at once. There is a certain uniformity to the palimp-sest, created by all the minor discrepancies and divergences. Micro-heterogeneity is revealed, in the aggregate, to be simply a busy kind of homo-geneity. While our individual eyeballs will never match up into one single mediated gaze—the bloodshot Cyclops of the Mass—they neverthe-less, in effect, combine into traceable searchlights, sweeping over the mediascape and illuminating the virtual maps of the Spectacle. This is partly what Guy Debord meant in describing the Spectacle as "diffuse." Where once the visual media's self-appointed role was to coerce a kind of higher-order synchronization among spectators and consumers—"the integrated Spectacle"—the evolution and specialization of communications media effectively began to *fragment* the collec-tive hegemony of the instrumentalized image (whether this be Brezhnev or Mickey Mouse). Given the rhizomatic nature of the Internet, the center cannot hold. But rather than lament this fact, the entrepreneurs have turned a crisis into an opportunity. The Spectacle disintegrates for strategic reasons. And a surreptitious centralization effect holds sway.[37]

In a sense, the rather monolithic notion of "the attention economy" divides and evolves into different attention *ecologies*, each with its own ecosystem and microclimate. As political philosopher Jason Read reminds us, *attention* cannot be read in the same way as *labor*, from a Marxist perspective. This is because capital doesn't really care who is doing the work, as long as it is being done. When it comes to attention, however, "*who* pays attention matters as much as clicks or time on site to those who track it, making it difficult to impose the sort of standardization of attention that any abstracting and quantifying requires. . . . Though there are ways to hold attention, trending topics and memes have broken the old 15 minutes of fame down to the microsecond. Attention must be constantly reconstituted in the present."[38] Read thus helpfully reminds us (via the work of Yves Citton) that attention is an unstable object, fluctuating between a resource, a faculty, a target, and an ideal, depending on the agenda of the discourse invoking it. But rather than being something which lives and dies in the individual, Read locates attention as "the contingent product of changing relations between individuals, collectivities, technological conditions, and social habits." In other words, it emerges within a specific (media) ecology: an insight that allows the discussion to avoid being reduced to an essentially moral critique of the psychological subject (i.e., someone who, for whatever reason, can never pay *enough* attention to what *really matters*).

Given the speed with which information passes through us, however, the very integrity of the concept of attention begins to disintegrate, along with the Spectacle that it used to focus on with such intensity. We live in an era—and a sociotechnical environment—in which we can share a joke, a family photo, a recipe, an amber alert, and news of a fresh massacre, all in the space of sixty seconds, and without any detectable emotional variance. We process and pass on information, running through us like Olestra. And yet these info-nuggets must leave some kind of psychosomatic residue as they pass through. Are we being "attentive" when we navigate the pixels flying at us with such autistic efficiency? Or are we almost intuitively, or semi-consciously, node-surfing, like a near-future William Gibson character who can recognize patterns in the network provided he or she doesn't actually try to focus on anything *in particular*?

4

NSFW:
The Fappening,
and Other Erotic Distractions

In the dwindling hours of August 2014, an unknown hacker—or group of hackers—released a giant freight of personal photographs of female celebrities, in various states of undress, onto the unsavory image-board 4chan. And within hours the Internet lit up like a horny Christmas tree. These images had been stolen from the phones of some unfortunate starlets, phones made especially vulnerable due to the Apple iPhone's cloud feature, which backs up all data "out there"—online. Testosterone-infused social media hubs, like Reddit, scrambled to assemble and itemize all the images, even as commentators tried to publicly shame anyone who looked at the intimate photos as accomplices to the crime. Certainly this *was* a crime, and there is much to be said about the gendered violence of (unconsenting) exposure on the Internet. But it should also not surprise us if this becomes a more common occurrence in the future, given the ways in which our portable and networked devices have become intimate and indispensable companions in our erotic lives. The notorious and ubiquitous selfie—whether fully clothed or completely naked—is the default currency of "digital natives," who circulate such auto-referential images through supposedly secure applications like Snapchat (in which the image is said to evaporate into the electronic ether, within a matter of seconds).[39] Thus, while post-millennial "cybersex" may not be as futuristic as we imagined back in the 1990s, the mating rituals of our age are indeed absolutely dependent on technological forms of mediation.

At the time of writing, Tinder is the most pop-ular and typical instance of this state of affairs. This dating app invites users to swipe left or swipe right, depending on an almost instant appraisal of someone's dating profile photo. No question, this is a particularly brutal form of responding to the visage of another human being: indeed, it is Emmanuel Levinas's nightmare. Instead of an infinite measure of care and obligation to the face of the other, as Levinas counseled, we have a sneering or smirking dismissal within a nanosecond of ersatz exposure to someone's singular, yet now homogenized, presence. As users of Tinder or similar applications, we are apt to be summarily banished by a capricious decision based on the most reductionist formula imaginable for conveying the complex aggregate of our perplexed existence (or, conversely, we are likely to be favored for equally fleeting and spurious reasons). This present-day scenario was a future that social theorist Erich Fromm hoped to save us from with his book *The Art of Love,* first published in 1956. In this often pessimistic diagnosis of the increasing convergence between our romantic lives and consumerist habits after World War II, Fromm argued that social interactions were beginning to occur according to the lineaments of "the personality market" (3). For Fromm, "the deepest need of man . . . is the need to overcome his separateness, to leave the prison of his aloneness" (8). But the always risky process of reaching out to our fellow human being, in the name of love, is now further complicated by the commercialization of attraction and the spectacularization of desire. Writing with an ongoing resonance, Fromm warns of the conformity this situation encourages, since "the aim is to belong to the herd" (13). Why? Because "if I am like everybody else, if I have no feelings or thoughts which make me different, if I conform in custom, dress, ideas, to the pattern of the group, I am saved; saved from the frightening experience of aloneness" (13) (an observation that accounts for the compulsory use of Mac laptops or the wearing of Abercrombie and Fitch clothing in certain large sectors of society). This "increasing tendency for the elimination of differences" (14) helps ensure that our sometimes awkward, stubborn, or ill-fitting subjectivities do not gum up the machine—especially the work-machine—since

> Modern capitalism needs men who co-operate smoothly and in large numbers; who want to consume more and more; and whose tastes are standardized and can be easily influenced and anticipated. It needs men who feel free and independent, not subject to any authority or principle or conscience—yet willing to be commanded, to do what is expected of them, to fit into the social machine without friction; who can be guided

without force, led without leaders, prompted without aim—except the one to make good, to be on
the move, to function, to go ahead. (85)

Such men (and women) can be trusted to restrict
themselves within the rather bare branches of
capitalist decision trees, because they can no
longer see the broader forest for such digital
timber.[40] Instead, "they can exchange their 'personality packages' and hope for a fair bargain"
(87). According to Fromm, we ourselves have
become as modular as the data sets and Northern
European furniture we sit on (or stand next to).

Sounding a lot like Stiegler, Fromm defines love
as "*the active concern for the life and the growth of
that which we love*" (26). While Tinder is designed
more for the quick millennial equivalent of the
old 1960s "zipless fuck" than long-lasting love,
all the apps and websites dedicated to "dating"—
wherever they happen to fall along the erotic
spectrum—exist within the same general libidinal
economy: one in which the "unit" of exchange
is not the nuanced and multifaceted expressions
of self, but the individual "personality package"
that horrified Fromm more than half a century
ago. This package that represents all the corners

of our being is determined by the template of the app or site: name, occupation, interests, connections, profile picture, and so on. One must adapt to the reductive parameters of the program in order to show up on the collective radar. In this way, a form of "bleeding" occurs between different hubs that aspire to different services, tones, and clientele. Whether we are logging on to a dating site for farmers, sailors, Christian singles, pagan polyamorites, or bored husbands and wives looking for an affair—or some combination of the above—the personality packages can be processed the same way by the user. "Pass . . . pass . . . yes . . . no . . . maybe." The medium is the message. And the medium allows, or rather requires, a swift sorting of human particles into different baskets, thereby obliging us to play the role of Maxwell's demon, in some kind of compulsive and capricious bio-thermodynamic shell game.

Many might say that this is how we behave in urban modernity in any case, whether it is online or in the real world. We make snap decisions and then act on them, no matter how ill-informed about or unjust toward our fellow human being. But in this case the "personality package" becomes as tradable as a baseball card. We can sling another's profile to a friend's phone as nonchalantly as we might give them a stick of gum. The cumulative effect—at least for a critic like Fromm—is that our potential life partner is initially approached in the same way, through the same reified grids, as an online commodity. (Indeed, from this perspective, LinkedIn is really just Yelp for friends and colleagues.) The website Hot or Not, which invites users to submit photos of themselves, or others, to be instantly down- or up-voted based simply on a single image, exposes the dominant stock-market approach to (inter) personal status, value, and worth. We ourselves are judged on the criteria of ever-fluctuating virtual exchange value, measured online and in real time.

No wonder the line between self-exposure, in the hope of finding love, and amateur pornography, in the hope of finding *jouissance*, is so often crossed on such sites. The difference between OK Cupid, where one might possibly find one's "other half," and Pornhub, where one might find a badly lit simulation of one's most secret kink, is not as stark or certain as we might like to think. Why settle for a flawed human being

when there are so many others out there, throb-
bing just out of life's current frame, with pure
potentiality? Who can compete with the sheer
mass of "others" out there, with better bodies,
haircuts, clothes, salaries, postures, anecdotes,
apartments, friends, health plans, and vacation
options? No wonder we live our lives in a state of
erotic distraction. Or rather, no wonder we live
our lives in a state of distraction that promises the
erotic and yet leaves us all too often mired in the
simply sexual (according to Marcuse's law that
hypersexualization leads quickly and inevitably to
de-eroticization).[41]

In classrooms and blog posts, we are likely
to hear smart people in their twenties claiming
that dating apps are more "efficient" than older
modes of arranging an intimate encounter. Given
the challenges young people face—shadowed by
debt, and trying to balance studying, working,
and/or the demands of life—this kind of sexual
pragmatism makes perfect sense. But a social
system which leaves so little *time* to experience
serendipitous, bodily encounters, originating
in the public sphere, does not bode well for
the psyche of those now obliged to treat their
romantic or erotic life like a quick trip to the

mall. The acceleration of intimacy, facilitated by social media, will no doubt have a profound impact on our notions of Eros, identity, and cultural ideas about the search for love. Badiou, for example, states that "love always starts with an encounter. And . . . this encounter [has] the quasi-metaphysical status of an *event*, namely of something that doesn't enter into the immediate order of things" (28). Žižek, for his part, extends this logic into the world of online dating, leading him to lament the loss of the authentic encounter in an age where lovers are introduced by specially tailored algorithms, rather than by the random nature of life, or the whim of the Fates. "The process of engaging in emotional relations is increasingly organized along the lines of a market relationship," Žižek writes.

> Such a procedure relies on self-commodification: for internet dating or marriage agencies, prospective partners present themselves as commodities, listing their qualities and posting their photos. What is missing here is what Freud called *der einzige Zug*, that singular pull which instantly makes me like or dislike the other. Love is a choice that is experienced as necessity. At a certain point, one is

overwhelmed by the feeling that one already *is* in love, and that one cannot do otherwise. By definition, therefore, comparing qualities of respective candidates, deciding with whom to fall in love, cannot be love. This is the reason why dating agencies are an anti-love device *par excellence* (92).

Perhaps such thinking, however, comes from an older generation who do not understand or appreciate the new *habitus* of digital media, and thus discount the possibility that such "events" are perfectly capable of occurring within the serendipities of online interactions: coded or not. (After all, any initial encounter between lovers during the twentieth century was apt to happen within, between, around, or through technical and commercial networks or spaces.) The experience of online dating, or matchmaking, is still open to the caprices of timing, mood, and other contingencies—even as it is highly influenced by an algorithm. The encounter or event that Badiou and Žižek mourn may yet occur in the unstable, underdetermined experience of the initial exchanges (just as true love can blossom within the restricted parameters of an arranged marriage or blind date). This is the thing about the event: it can explode onto the scene from the most unexpected of places and in the most surprising ways. The wider hope is thus that we can use new technologies to further focus, refine, and reinvent the inherently *technical* nature of erotic communication—thus breaking the humanist spell of our most cherished, and crippling, romantic discourses—while also avoiding the risks of outsourcing our libidos to forces that are only interested in what Marcuse called "the performance principle" (or what Frank Pasquale calls "the algorithmic self").

Social media is inherently libidinal, to the degree that we participate in it in order to be recognized, endorsed, verified, or, if one is more a voyeur than an exhibitionist, to find objects of cathexis and fetishism. Tumblr and its ilk have rendered all aspects of life pornographic, in the sense that we consume foodporn, artporn, architectureporn, dataporn, carporn, natureporn, and so on, even if we don't seek out images of naked humans. In her book *Why Internet Pornography Matters*, feminist philosopher Margret Grebowicz argues that the mode of transmission is more significant than the content when discussing desire in the digital context. Indeed, today's online erotica is "qualitatively different" from its previous incarnations in print and on film or television screens. "What is striking about Internet pornography," she writes, "in contrast to previous forms of hard-core moving-image pornography, is the meta-level discourse of information sharing in which it is situated. There is something about the imaginary of democratized information that immediately makes it porn-friendly, or that at the very least makes people take off their clothes" (51). Indeed: "pornography is problematic, not because a certain kind of image causes its consumer to commit a certain kind of act, or because this imagery produces gender-as-inequality, or that it distorts the truth of normal sexuality. It is problematic as an instrument of the kind of democracy that requires the disappearance of the secret existence and the auto-intoxication of the social.[42] Given its success, Internet porn is arguably the most important tool of a social order which requires transparency of its subjects" (58).[43]

The very term *Internet pornography* becomes increasingly redundant, as all things obliged to appear in our browsers and on our screens are domesticated, visible, available, "taggable." This attitude toward an object falls under the regime of what Heidegger called *vorstellen* [to represent or conceive]: an unprecedented modern mode of viewing that approaches its object in terms of *calculated possession*. What the (increasingly controversial) German philosopher saw as one of the decisive and fundamental revolutions in the history of knowledge—the "conquest of the world as picture"—mutates even further, as the social world fragments into a sea of solitary solipsisms. The world picture is no longer the Earth framed by satellite imagery, but an endless parade of earthlings made available for scopic consumption: all within the scene of the personal world we (feel we) create and configure on our screens. The sense of mastery we get from tapping, rotating, *examining* whatever pops up in front of us gives us the feeling of grasping a given thing: if not in a haptic way, then in a putatively deeper sense that gets to the coded bones of the object. We grasp its *abstract essence*. Which in turn allows us to zoom in or swipe it away with God-like omnipotence inside the personal universe of our interface. For a Heideggerian, however (presuming some still exist), the price we pay for this illusion of complete agency toward "the world" is the loss of true traction with the unique presence of any given other. While we may find some *attraction* to an avatar of a potential date, for instance, we cannot (yet) find any real *traction* with them, because we are *dis-tracted* by the power of the device which gives us the illusion of access to another's being. Or, in Heidegger's rather maddening and idiosyncratic language: "Representing is no longer the apprehending of that which presences, within whose unconceal-ment apprehending itself belongs, belongs indeed as a unique kind of presencing toward that which presences that is unconcealed" (149). Or in other words, the "birth to presence"—which makes up the event of authentic co-belonging—arrives stillborn, because our capacity to truly receive or register the alterity and facticity of the other has been destroyed by the medium that pretends to connect us (but in fact leaves us floating in our own techno-*umwelt*).

The ancient, Western distinction (and hierar-chy) between essence and appearance, however, seems to have reversed in the age of the Internet: as if the magnetic poles of our own understand-ing of the universe have flipped. Today, the very status of something as having value is determined by its digital appearance, and all things that are not in the database wink into irrelevance or even nonexistence. This is the ontology of Google and other local search engines. If you don't show up in a "search," then your very actuality is at question. (Hence the disconcerting moment when the person we are talking with in real life confesses that she or he does not have a Facebook account, and we suddenly suspect that we have been having a conversation with a ghost.)[44]

This is where hypersynchronization reenters the picture, since we addicts of social media are all maintaining our profiles and our digital ecosystems as diligently as the grounds-keeping staff of a gated community's golf course. And yet, some of us are curating recipes while others are collecting vintage toys. Some are assembling signatures to protest a proposed legislation, while others are combing through those very same signatures for targeted marketing campaigns. We all step into the same coverless "book" but remain on different pages. Even the millions of users of a porn aggregation site soon find themselves splintered into niche interests, which further fractalize into surreal diagrams of the Internet's schizophrenic Id. The World Wide Web thrives on Freud's "narcissism of minor differences." Of course, it is impossible to imagine what "being on the same page" would look like when considering a population greater than the average classroom, let alone the sum of people on the planet. And yet Stiegler's key term does assume a certain uniformity of attention or experience. The very notion of hypersynchronization rests on our increasing co-distraction, captured and channeled by the program industries. Yet Stiegler himself wavers between prioritizing the *object* or *means* of distraction: that is to say, whether such a funneling process is due to something like the response to a terrorist attack (which is specifically located in time and space), or instead, the technical frame and apparatus that compels and restricts our modes of attention. The former could not happen on the scale that it now does without the latter, so we must prioritize this in our schemata, even as we recognize the dialectic between them. (Why would we continue to log on if it weren't for certain crystallizing "events" for us to use as an alibi to share, comment, and respond to?)

When it comes to the almost daily scenario of something like leaked celebrity nudity—with or without permission—we may click on the beckoning link or not, depending on factors varying from boredom levels to hormonal blood-sugar ratios. The remarkable thing, however, about the mass release of unauthorized nude photos of female stars in the middle of 2014 is that—for better or for worse—it stands as one of those moments when a vast majority of those online were thinking about, and responding to, the same "event"—at least for the limited attention span of a twenty-four-hour news cycle. (And this was all the more notable given that this wasn't a giant corporate-sponsored event, like the World Cup final or the Olympic Games.) Whether this response was disgust or titillation, or a combination of both, the Internet seemed to be, however briefly, "hypersynchronized," in Stiegler's sense: all tweeting, commenting, and arguing, in a figurative sense, "together." Our collective attention had been kettled and monopolized by this event, thanks to the incentivizing architecture of the social web: an event that onanistic young men had punningly dubbed "the fappening." The name here is significant, since it suggests a convergence between masturbation and a liminal moment in time: the kind of moment that cultures crave to release them from the tedium of relentlessly secular temporality. This was dubbed a "happening" which you could fap to. What more would a typical social media user want?! In a world of meaningless, simulated "events," *this*—for a split second—felt like something approaching a *real* one, since it was unintended and unexpected: seemingly the very opposite of a PR move. (And yet the cynics might rightly wonder, given the way a strategically released sex tape can now kick-start a new career or revive a flagging one.)

The sad thing, of course, is that a genuine event, like the WikiLeaks dump of the Snowden documents, or the Chelsea Manning files, is rendered equivalent to something as trivial as the so-called *fappening*. Geopolitics is trumped by celebrity, in the age of the military-industrial-entertainment complex. Indeed, as I write, the alleged hacking of Sony Pictures by North Korea, supposedly in protest at the release of the dude-comedy film *The Interview*, is creating more outrage than the Senate's damning findings concerning the U.S. administration's vast, secret, and system-atic torture program. Editorials and think pieces about this scandalous human rights violation were indeed passed around the networks as well. But here we see hypermodulation—or, deliber-ately deployed dissonance—in particularly clear outline. In this case, like in so many others, our attention wavers back and forth between two very different types of naked bodies. One shows a pale starlet, awkwardly trying to take a photo of her own bare buttocks in the bathroom mirror. The other shows an American soldier "rectally feeding" a dark-skinned prisoner in an unknown location. Even if one eschews looking at either image, out of principle or self-care, the fact that they both exist and are the topics of global chatter makes social media the site of a vertiginous lurching between their two scopic economies: so different in content, and yet sharing an unsettling affinity.

As long as the libido continues to be fracked for every last kilojoule of energy and attention, we will keep being confronted with desultory "fappenings" that—whether intentional or not—distract from the struggle between disclosure and redaction with which the people of real power are involved.

Conclusion

Chasing the Unicorn

In the world of critical theory, it is a vocational habit—when seeking to sum up The Current Situation—to interpret the wreckage of the present through Paul Klee's *Angelus Novus*, as described by Walter Benjamin: a fearful winged figure, blowing backward through the ever-unfolding catastrophe of history. In this case, however, we might turn to a different painting by Klee, finished two years later in 1922, and thus, in a sense, a creative gift bestowed on us *after* the end of history. This painting depicts largely featherless avian creatures, attached to a thin wire, which is itself connected to a hand crank. The legs and torsos of these highly abstract birds are as thin as the wire they are perched upon, and could even conceivably be extensions of it. Their provenance seems neither entirely organic nor completely mechanical. These are cyborg creatures that apparently sing at the turning of a handle (although no guiding hand comes into the picture). Some kind of pit or coffin, lit soft pink from within, seems to await beneath them, patient for the moment they drop off the perch. One art critic has described the painting as allegorically depicting mechanically captured animals, "their heads flopping in exhaustion and pathos." Furthermore, "one bird's tongue flies up out of its beak, an exclamation point punctuating its grim fate—to chirp under compulsion" (96).[45] The title of the painting—as if Klee had an uncanny premonition of our mechanized future from nearly a century ago—is *The Twittering Machine*. Indeed, we would be hard-pressed to find a better image to represent the present age, in which a rapidly increasing majority "chirp under compulsion"—for work, for publicity, for our own obscure psychosomatic motives. (John Cage's famous quote, "I have nothing to say—and I'm saying it," doesn't seem nearly so profound in the age of Facebook and Twitter.)

The twittering machine of (a)social media has given us a rather birdlike aspect, as our heads jerk and tilt, trying to see who just pinged or poked us, as we peck at the screens, in an attempt to find pellets of mental nourishment or encouragement. If information is "a difference that makes a difference," as Bateson famously defined it, then we are certainly not experiencing information overload but quite the contrary. Rather, we find ourselves assaulted by noise, bereft of signal. And this constant splicing of the spectrum of our attention is starting to physically damage our neurological selves.[46] (One begins to wonder if we should start to monitor the national deficit in terms of attention, in addition to international trade.) This intensified form of infinite distraction—only the blink of an eye in human history—is already having significant repercussions in terms of our understanding of what it means to be a person in a certain place, at a given moment in time. Human culture *is* intergenerational continuity (made up of what Stiegler calls "tertiary retentions"—the technological storage and transmission of collective memories[47]).The long threads that compose our group, and the individual identities from which they are woven, start to fray and wear away. As one commentator, Andrew Gallix, put it, "We live in an age of total recall and rampant dementia."[48] Google, Facebook, and Wikipedia now function as our hive-mind, reassembling itself anew in real time, according to the pressures of corporate sponsors and caprices of dubious gatekeepers. Every factoid one could imagine is catalogued somewhere on the Internet. Meanwhile, the program industries busy themselves with what Henry Giroux calls "the violence of organized forgetting"— that is, the concerted effort to make the people forget all the atrocities that have been occurring for several centuries now in "our" name, in the name of civilization and democracy, but which in bloody fact represent the absolute antithesis of such ideals.

The precious process of transindividuation— in which we dialectically distinguish ourselves from the mass, as a reflective personality, while simultaneously remaining a vector for the human collectivity (alive, dead, and not-yet born)—becomes threatened, no thanks to our increasingly goldfish-like mnemonic capacities and squirrelish attention spans. When our responses are preempted and shaped by the

protocols of the network—"only 140 characters
. . . only 'like' button option . . . only memes or
emojis accepted"—then our critical faculties start
to follow the same subroutines as the algorithm.
Ping goes the phone. Jerk goes the neck. Our
latent Pavlovian vulnerabilities rise to the surface,
exploited by those who have entire armies of sci-
entists—social and cognitive—at their bidding,
paid handsomely to keep us monkeys holding the
electronic bananas, without realizing it's a trap.[49]

Compulsion. Distraction. Procrastination.
Addiction. The four courses of the apocalypse.

As one (virtual) friend of mine posted recently
on Facebook: "What we need is an expressive
platform where we can embrace our most intimate attempts at free self-expression that will
slowly become habitual so that any sort of action
in the world that might cause a singular reac-
tion and reflex will become only more fodder
for expressing 'ourselves' in a digital public in
a manner that leaves precisely no room for any
novel or singular response... oh..? facebook? what?
you already have bought that patent? oh? we are
producing it for you? ok. thanks."[50] Our collective expression, once known as *the commons*, is
now elicited and encircled by private interests

and technologies (what Mark Andrejevic calls "the digital enclosure"). Our thoughts, conversations, memories, artifacts are instantly owned by others—expropriated—once we upload them into the network. Our faces, tagged and databased. All our interactions are captured, channeled, reprocessed, and returned to us, in a giant feedback loop that coils ever tighter in an effort to persuade us to forget that there are other, non-patented, forms of communication out there. From this perspective, we may begin to change our minds and consider *The Human Centipede*, and not *The Twittering Machine*, as the most accurate figure or allegory for social media: a horrifying daisy chain of unwitting people, all stitched together, mouth-to-anus, swallowing the various excretions of our fellow men and women, without being able to draw breath or sustenance from any other source.

Certainly, existing is no picnic. Freud lists the three main ways that we try to cope with the burden of consciousness: "powerful distractions," "substitutive satisfactions," and "intoxicating substances" (41). Social media combines all three survival strategies, if we consider the digital habit as itself a mind-altering addiction. But from this perspective, culture or civilization can be viewed as little more than a moral hierarchy of ways to distract ourselves from the inevitability of our own death and of those we love. Indeed, it may be more difficult than we think—explaining to an alien anthropologist why running our eyes over black lines in an object called a "book" is considered far superior to tracing our eyes around a screen depicting an object called a "videogame." After a while, the laments of the keepers of old media start to sound like they are simply saying, "Your delusional coping mechanism isn't as good as my delusional coping mechanism." We may have to seriously consider that such distinctions are a matter of opinion and learned aesthetics. But the fact is that our coping mechanisms are becoming rusty, and at an increasing rate than before (no doubt thanks to the effects of climate change).

The planet is in trouble, and social media is where the majority of us have decided to bury our heads. Just as ostriches are said to indulge in this form of denial, California has thoughtfully provided us with seemingly endless buckets of silicon to do the same. And yet nothing is end-less, of course. Our resources are as finite as our lives, albeit exhausting themselves at a different rate. Email gives us the comforting illusion that we are saving trees. But the energy needed to power the networks within which emails circulate also decimates the environment. So we are trapped in a vicious cycle. The world is demoralizing, depressing, and stress-inducing. And so we seek distractions from it: distractions that further aggravate the conditions which make it so difficult to cope with in the first place. New media, or rather the economic system within which current new media are framed and maintained, create a surplus anxiety, above and beyond the baseline existential angst of being human, wrenched from the cosmic continuum and fallen into the fate of individuality.

This is why Stiegler refers to technology as the *pharmakon*. It is a cure for loneliness and surplus anxiety. But only at a certain (uncertain) dose. At a given point, the cure becomes a poison. (A reversal of Heidegger's "danger which saves" ... in this case, technology is the *savior which harms*.) Certainly, our appetite for distraction is not a healthy one. It is bulimic. We go on Netflix binges without knowing how to purge. Our souls become obese, along with our bodies, if we mistake the proprietary formula for "social" life for the kind created in common (and in the commons). In his *Symposium*, Plato noted that "the interests of rulers require that their subjects should be poor in spirit and that there should be no strong bond of friendship or society among them" (499). By this account, our rulers have done a very sound job of ensuring such a situation, as friendship becomes far more fleeting, promiscuous, and provisional than it once was: a "liquid" form of companionship (Bauman), assembled and undone via modem or satellite.

The indispensable sixth sense—the sense of potential—which, at different times, crackled off the streets or inside book covers; has been blocked out by advertising billboards.[51] "Hope"—or, rather, what Lauren Berlant calls cruel optimism—now occurs in the banal imagination of brandspace (something no human can ever access, no matter how many Prada shoes one has). Of course, this is not a black-and-white situation. The so-called "Luddite position"[52] is impotent, and helps soothe only the wounded souls of the self-selected special ones. Even Heidegger understood that we cannot go back to the garden. (And as Graham Harman has said, "Nature is not natural and can never be naturalized" [251].) But we are abdicating our responsibility to ourselves and future generations (and here I'm not only talking about humans) if we choose to simply focus on the positive aspects of social media and the kind of scattered subjectivity it encourages. Yes, there are brilliant things about new, networked technologies. Our lives have been enriched by them. Beautiful friendships, enriching encounters, spectacular love affairs, important knowledges, and inspiring artworks have been conceived, conducted, and created through them. But this does not absolve us of the need to take careful and sustained note of the corrosive aspects. The absurd fairy tale of "the red pill" in *The Matrix* in fact contains a useful allegory for *seeing through* the overcoded environments we are invited to inhabit: environments we are cleverly convinced to not question, or redesign for our own purposes, beyond the profitable options pre-provided for us.[53]

In a certain sense, it doesn't even make sense to posit a space or place, distinct from elsewhere, called "digital media," since the line between on- and offline has been practically erased thanks to mobile technologies and the loss of such partitioning in our thinking. We inhabit the möbius strip, following the plane of digital interaction seamlessly into analog interconnections and back again. Or, rather, these happen simultaneously, 24/7. This doesn't mean we should nostalgically romanticize the world before the Internet, as if people were organically more considerate or intelligent or empathetic. One casual glance at the twentieth century will put a lie to that little fantasy. Friends were not necessarily more satisfying presences, simply because they were in the same room (something Madame de Sévigné noted in the seventeenth century, in her celebrated letters, making reference to those tiresome people who "deprive us of solitude without affording us company" [in Proust 11]). This does not mean, however, that we should swallow the toxic froth of the digital cheerleaders of a techno-utopian near-future.

We began this book with a vision of bots, reading our updates more diligently than we do ourselves. Automated online activity rivals our own, as our machines click, whistle, and fraternize. Multimedia artist and theorist Hito Steyerl sees hope in the sheer volume of "image spam" flooding the networks. For Steyerl, the media ecology has evolved, so that we are no longer so much amused to death but "represented to pieces."[54] She thus argues that the tsunami of stock images, depicting perfectly Photoshopped models, provides the cover for us *real*, flawed humans to embark on a new exodus, since they are doing the thankless work of the Spectacle for us. "What if actual people," she writes, " . . . were not excluded from spam advertisements because of their assumed deficiencies but had actually chosen to desert this kind of portrayal? What if image spam thus became a record of a widespread refusal, a withdrawal of people from representation?" But even this feels like an ironic messianic program predating the "digital prom-ise" (Andrejevic) of prosumer involvement. Were we to update Steyerl's brilliant provocation, we might talk instead of—or as well of—a global "withdrawal from *participation*." A refusal to interact (which was always only a form of coun-terfeit participation, in any case). A capacity to resist click bait.[55]

Such a refusal might be a conscious deployment of what Galloway, Thacker, and Wark have recently called "excommunication": a mode of mediation that eschews bi-directionality (10). "One cannot help notice in our media cultures," they write, "the seduction of empty messages, flitting here and there like so many angelic constellations in the aether" (10). If we grant the argument that "for every communication there is a correlative excommunication," then we might well ponder the possibility that even our most profound exchanges turn out, in the long view, to be essentially phatic. The medium is the message, and the message is "there are no more messages," just signals without meaning. Which is not to advocate for a worldwide Bartleby strategy (although that surely couldn't hurt), but to think with this trio, in terms of approaching mediation as something more complicated—and ultimately more dysfunctional, and ontologically unsettling—than a technique of communication. The distraction afforded by the incessant twittering of our social media is thus not simply a matter of digital decoys, pointing us away from more enfranchised, empowered sociopolitical models, but a new global experiment in amplifying the nihilistic ex-communication of modern life. (To paraphrase Derrida: "There is nothing outside the texting.")

But this would take a different book to unpack properly. Instead, we conclude with the concept of hypermodulation: the attempt to distract us from the fact that we are indeed being synchronized to an unprecedented degree. When the Internet first burst into the popular imagination, people feared the atomization of public life. Why would we congregate in the modern agoras of the *polis* if we could hang out virtually with small cliques who think and feel as we do? Moreover, publishers and producers of all kinds feared the end of the best seller or the box office smash, since everyone would be enjoying—perhaps even *making*—their own personal micro-niches and customized genre hybrids. Fast-forward a couple of decades, and this concern—that the social fabric would dissolve into individual tastes and a galaxy of options—appears more than a little ill-founded. Indeed, while it is true that we can explore all kinds of eccentric offerings we didn't have easy access to before, the configuration of social media has meant that we still drift toward the more heavily sponsored commodities in vast numbers. The world, it seems, will never want for easy conversation fodder. Whether this is because we are worker bees for the honey of well-marketed products and events, or because we, as a species, feel the need for a shared point of reference in order to communicate the fact that we don't have much to say to each other, is something of a circular question.

When Eric Garner was killed by a New York City police officer in 2014, after being placed in a banned choke hold, social media lit up with the hashtag #blacklivesmatter. At least in the liberal networks to which I have access, the scandal accompanying this fatality, as one emblematic of too many others, and the subsequent whitewash of justice and accountability, led to several weeks of remarkably focused online discourse and interaction. Protests were quickly organized and assembled. The people flickered back into being, summoned into existence by the urgency and atrocity of the situation. (As Steyerl writes, the people "are an event, which might happen one day.") And yet, even before this collective anger was diluted by the passing of time and the introduction of new, less troubling, memes, social media connections were hypermodulating themselves, and others, away from a *potentially effective* form of grass-roots hypersynchronization. "I'm just going to put this video of a kitten falling asleep here, as some welcome relief to all the trouble on the wires tonight." So wrote many well-meaning people, indulging in an Internet ritual known as "the unicorn chaser" (following up some unpleasant or disturbing news with a cute or distractingly fanciful image or idea). To clarify, I am not condemning the instinct—perhaps even the need—to "break the tension," as a psychological failing (although it is certainly a political one). Instead, it is to draw attention to the ways in which staccato *affects* are embedded in social media: a situation that gels perfectly with the interests of those who hope any attempt to break out beyond virtual interventions will have no *effect*. Once again, indignation is rerouted around the network, so that it doesn't reach critical mass and explode.[56]

Is distraction the problem, then? Is the solution simply to pay better attention to important things, and install better personal filters to screen out the trivial and inconsequential? Such a conclusion would be condescending, simplistic, and unrealistic.[57] Silly memes are not the problem. An economic system that provides silly memes as pellets toward enduring another day of work is the problem. Here I can't help but largely agree with Adorno, who wrote the following in a letter to Walter Benjamin in 1936: "The theory of distraction [*Zerstreuung*] does not, despite its shocking seduction, completely convince me. If only for the simple reason that in the communist society work will be organized such that people will no longer be so tired and so dulled as to need entertainment [*Zerstreuung*]" (in North 146). Interestingly, and counter-intuitively, distraction was not a simple foe or challenge for Benjamin. The process first detailed by Kant, in which we receive, convert, and synthesize the multi-sensual signals of the universe for our limited, human understanding (known as "apperception"), can become complicated in a generative way by distraction. Or so Benjamin believed. A new medium like film thus had the historically unique capacity to "disrupt" traditional, relatively organic, apperception; striking its structure and rewiring its filters and sensors. Paul North describes it like this: "In becoming a habit, distraction becomes a tool for dissolving regimes of thought, modes of understanding, by admitting an empirical moment into the transcendental structure of apperception" (164–65). In other words, distraction can break habits of thinking, being, and acting, which themselves have worked in tandem to foreclose new opportunities. We might then propose the possibility, or project, of fostering a *centripetal* form of distraction (i.e., as something more enmeshed than sheer dispersal, allowing a self-reflexive type of engagement which avoids the overdetermined mode of experience known as *attention*). We might be confident in presuming that Benjamin would not have dismissed social media as the latest opium of the masses, but rather as the digital arcades of the multitude—both promising and camouflaging new democratic possibilities, new interpersonal configurations, and new collective sensibilities. Just as we are not to simply mourn the shattering of the aura by the novel technologies of reproduction, we should resist lamenting the shattering of attention by the new technologies of interaction. But this does not mean we should simply welcome the new (anti-)temporalities these systems create, especially the lack of time given to receive, reflect, and respond.

What would this enabling form of distraction look like? It's very hard to say. Diagnostic studies all too often falter at the point of envisaging an exit strategy. But it could indeed involve a distraction from distraction—a meta-distraction—that wouldn't take us back to a quasi-religious focus on the Good, but instead open up the range of encounters, beyond those provided by our official Internet providers (the same ones who might very well soon be renamed experience providers). For North, this would be a "revitalized concept of primal distraction," before it became the whipping post of a modern disciplinary society. "Distraction is the condition of possibility for a political event: a dense diaspora" (165)—just as the distracted person is an "enabler of a politics without being-with" (73). Certainly, it would take another book to explore this intriguing and creative progressive vision of this culturally loaded term. Suffice it to say here that distraction is indeed too complicated and rich a discourse to simply be used as an opportunity to condemn. After all, distractions from tedious jobs, themselves created for no reason other than to distract from the great ongoing Ponzi scheme of capitalism, cannot be considered harmful or undesirable. And for North, distraction is a specific mode of receptivity, with its own kind of promiscuous attunement. Indeed, rethinking distraction

suggests not just the possibility but the existence of an infinitely inclusive collective without the need to count out its members or represent itself, on the model of the communality of *le distrait*, which is furthermore neither revolutionary nor utopian. It refuses the time signatures of both these dreams; it is something less than to dream, to quote Kant. It is not "to come." Although we cannot know this, it is already here. It does not require, for its grouping principle, any ground for being-with, since it is infinitely dispersed historically, conceptually, and perhaps geographically. . . . [Distraction also] suggests a way to think of structural change in politics that does not depend on the fiction of a historical continuum, or even its interruption. Distraction breaks the contract between thought and time, even though it says nothing about what steps in if and when people regain their senses. (183)

We should accept this challenge to rethink distraction as a potential ally. And we should likewise consider the implications of breaking the "contract between thought and time." Clearly, multitasking is here to stay, as are the ever-new networked modes of mediation. As seductive as the notion of unplugging is, along with calls for a "slow thought" movement, such notions can only function as the Romantic shadow to the cynical hijacking of technics by those deeply invested in what Steven Shaviro calls "plundernomics."

Certainly we shall *always* exhibit an appetite for distraction. The challenge is to become more mindful of the ways in which such an appetite is both sated and stimulated by the standardized forces of monopolized convenience. Synchronization is an issue when it means the capacity to think, act, and be otherwise atrophies. But synchronization is to be welcomed, and produced, when it works against what Giroux calls "the disimagination machine." That is, when it can be deployed against the channeling of focus away from injustice, inequality, corruption, and exploitation. In aesthetics, diversity. In an agenda for action, a fundamental accord (as the basis for a constellation of different, strategic responses).[58] Opting out of social media may be an effective strategy for some. Creating software held in common (and in the commons) may be another, along with a host of site- or event-specific interventions or subventions. The challenge is all the greater, however, to synchronize our watches, now that we tell time by smartphone, or by Apple's latest timepiece. (No doubt there is an app for that.) Indeed, the task is to recover the promise in Kracauer's critical and political insight concerning the media consumers of his own time, and the way this might resonate with those of our own. A people both gathered and dispersed, absorbed and distracted, "who so easily allow themselves to be stupefied only because they are so close to the truth."

Notes

1 As Geert Lovink asks: "How do we overcome this paradoxical era of hyped-up individualization that results precisely in the algorithmic outsourcing of the self?" (34).

2 For a more detailed account of this novel merger between decoy and distraction, see my piece "Look at the Bunny, Or What Roger Rabbit Can Tell Us about the Second Gulf War," in *Look at the Bunny: Totem, Taboo, Technology* .

3 This book considers Facebook as the default instance of social media (at the time of writing), for several reasons. One is that Facebook has the largest global user base of the main websites considered to be "social media" proper (i.e., with content powered by users). In early 2015, this was 1.39 billion *active* monthly users. As a result, Facebook has become the metonym for the phenomenon that used to be referred to as the Internet 2.0 (even as a large number of people use Facebook

while claiming not to even use the Internet). Mark Zuckerberg's company is also the most all-encompassing iteration of social media, in terms of the types of content found there and the variety of interactions that can be had (with the exception of Reddit, which, for historical reasons, has its own specific demographic tone). Finally, Facebook extends far beyond its own domain (name) by means of the applet embedded in millions of other webpages, not to mention the amorphous Facebook effect in the real world, where people are "on" the site, even when not, through sheer anticipation, imagination, or speculation—compulsively checking their phones for updates or responses. For all these reasons we can safely say that Facebook is, well, the *face* of social media—even as it will likely be replaced by another überhub in a few years' time.

4 For the most sophisticated recent treatment of this key term, see Paul North's *The Problem of Distraction*, a monograph which begins with the startling claim that "there is no distraction today, even though—and perhaps because—there are too many distractions" (175). Rather, there is "only an attention to the zero degree" (5). As North notes: "The English word calls up several images: a mathematics of division; a morality of bad choices; a movement of dispersion across a grid of more and more disparate points; a diminishment of strength, quality, or purity; vices or quasi-vices that produce pleasure without work; amusement, diversion, entertainment" (1–2). North skillfully teases out the theoretical paradoxes of the artificial dialectic between attention and its presumed opposite. "Attention

intensifies most," he writes, ". . . in its loss; it becomes itself when one goes in search of it. Producing itself out of fear of its unavailability . . . it must be pulled back continually from an unknown place to which it has slipped away" (2). As a consequence, the most we can say with confidence, in order to distinguish between the two states, is that "attention is not non-attention" (3). The problem ("distraction") is thus conceived as *both* a lack (of discipline, focus, etc.), and an excess (of attention to things that shouldn't matter). And the solution ("attention") is a positive faculty that reveals itself to be without content, when one tries to see it in action. The distraction/attention dyad cannot be prized apart, at least not without damaging both elements. Consider how we describe someone preoccupied with a gnawing, unspoken thought as being "distracted," even as they are clearly paying *too* much attention to something specific. Such descriptions betray the various hierarchies and moralisms embedded in the term. Distraction is thus consistently equated with paying attention *to the wrong things*. Like the deep-water kraken, attention can be *seen* or *captured* only in its lifeless state, hauled out of the ocean within which it functions. Thus "what we call distraction is attentive thought degraded until it can do nothing but clamor for a return to its ideal" (5). For North, the really interesting question is what distraction might become—what it might reveal to us—if we resist the habit of thinking of it as subordinate to the assumed plenitude and valued capacity of "full" attention (6), and thus indicating a neurological or moral failing. Distraction might then be thought as something more than another way of describing an attention deficit. Indeed, for North, earlier thinkers, such as La Bruyère, Kafka, Heidegger, Kracauer, and Benjamin, offer specific ways to approach distraction as something more enabling, more charged with potential, than being considered merely a symptom of personal incontinence.

5 Consistent with Bernard Stiegler's reading of technics as *pharmakon*—that is, as both disease and cure— we find the enlisting of technology to study the very symptoms created by an exponential increase in technological use. For instance, the *Atlantic* recently reported that "researchers at Princeton set out to build a tool that could show people what their brains are doing in real time, and signal the moments when their minds begin to wander. . . . [This "mind booster" machine could] change the way we think about paying attention—and even introduce new ways of treating illnesses like depression." See Taylor Beck, "The Attention Machine."

6 An important precursor to Stiegler's lexicon and system, especially in relation to key concepts like "synchronization," "the program industries," and "disorientation," is the seminal media theorist Vilém Flusser. One of Flusser's key concepts is the paradigmatic modern shift to a programmed society, in which humans increasingly become not only functionaries but *functions* of the generalized apparatus in the "posthistory" world. For Flusser, as for Stiegler, "*Apparatus always function increasingly independently from their programmer's intentions*" (25). Indeed, Flusser makes

note of the special role of instrumentalized distraction in such a situation, deploying "techniques that aim *to divert* our thought from particular subjects" (107). "We want maximum experience to accumulate sensations," he writes, "because in successive sensations we divert the consciousness of our alienation in relation to the world" (109). We are collaborators with "programmed life," meaning that "man is not only a being that produces instruments, but also a being that produces instruments in order to escape from the tension produced by his instruments" (131).

7 The following paragraphs are based on the discussion thread that ensued when I first posted the observation on Facebook that eventually grew into this book. One benefit of social media is having almost instant feedback, or "peer review," for hypotheses or speculations; and my thinking on this topic has been enriched by a phalanx of insightful and engaged critical theorists. I would thus like to thank in particular Karl Steel, Nicholas Birns, Bernard Dionysius Geoghegan, Marco Deseriis, Mohammed Salemy, and Ben Peters for chiming in and allowing me to poach and remix some of their thoughts and words into a collage for this new context.

8 In his short but potent critique, *24/7*, which describes a new global regime "beyond clock time," Jonathan Crary touches on Stiegler's key concept of hypersynchronization, noting that the philosopher "has written widely on the consequences of what he sees as the homogenization of perceptual experience within contemporary culture. He is especially concerned with the

global circulation of mass-produced 'temporal objects,' which, for him, include movies, television programs, popular music, and video clips" (50). While Crary shares such concerns, to an extent, he believes that this problem "is secondary to the larger systemic colonization of individual experience. . . . Most important now is not the capture of attentiveness by a delimited object—a movie, television program, or piece of music—whose mass reception seems to be Stiegler's main preoccupation, but rather the remaking of attention into repetitive operations and responses that always overlap with acts of looking or listening" (52). Thus, power no longer focuses on mass-deception, "but rather states of neutralization and inactivation, in which one is dispossessed of time" (88).

9 Given that language itself is considered to be an apparatus for Agamben, "escaping" the nefarious nets of technology could only mean rejecting our ostensible humanity altogether, and returning full circle to an absolutely inalienated state in the Open of our recovered animality. This romance of a (post)human animal to come, free from linguistically colonized thought, certifies Agamben as truly one of our most committed Luddites.

10 See, for instance, Kevin Bales, *Disposable People: New Slavery in the Global Economy*, which details the shameful structures that have only intensified in the ten years since this book's publication, given the accelerated race for mobile technologies.

11 See Steven Johnson's optimistic piece of counter-wisdom, *Everything Bad Is Good for You.*

12 I still vividly recall my mother's pained expression when she asked me to explain what this new Facebook phenomenon was, and how I used it, during the early days of its ascendancy into popular consciousness. "But why would you *expose* yourself like that?!" she asked in an exasperated tone, ashamed on my behalf for my now exponentially amplified lack of dignity.

13 See Lauren Berlant, "Faceless Book."

14 In Franco Berardi's terms, this is to perversely value the modern emphasis on *connection* over *conjunction*, where the former is less authentic because it is more reified than the latter. "Desire dwells in conjunction," he writes, "and is killed by connection. Connection means a relationship between formatted segments; making desingularized bodies compatible. Conjunction means singular, unrepeatable communication between round bodies. Connection means Integration of smooth bodies in a space which is no space and in a time which is no time" (98). In her resistance to the too-tempting narrative of decadence, Berlant slyly encourages us to create our own silver linings where perhaps there are none (i.e., in "mere" connections), and in doing so to project new possibilities into new patterns, free from old moralisms.

15 The fetishistic power of the smartphone has been effectively parodied by a prankster product called NoPhone, which is simply a black piece of plastic, the same size and dimensions as an iPhone. Like nicotine gum, this physical negation of the smartphone can help wean someone off their addiction, in this case to social media, just as its sheer opacity illuminates

145

the virtual hold and promise of our mobile devices as windows into alternative spaces.

16 It may be said that smartphones cultivate not *dasein*— "there-being"—but "neither-here-nor-there-being." They are the midwives of "the birth to distraction." Moreover, this will only be exacerbated further when digital displays become commonplace within the field of our regular vision, as first attempted with Google Glass. Early adopters of this technology, colloquially known as "glassholes," were instinctively distrusted for the very reason that they trouble ontological assumptions linking the body and the presence (interpersonal availability) of the person. As visibly "augmented" humans living fully online and offline at same time, or in the no-place (utopia) between them, glassholes violate a deep humanist principle of "being there"—which is one of the main reasons they often found themselves the target of great hostility, even beatings. (Neal Stephenson, in his earlier cyberpunk novels, called such techno-creatures "gargoyles," for their sinister tendency to watch over the world while not interacting "properly" with it.) We should not discount other motives for the hostility, however, including a healthy resistance to being so fully penetrated by patented technologies, and the hidden agendas they bring with them, like tiny Trojan horses. (Which is not to excuse violence perpetrated against individuals.) Nevertheless, just as the world at large used to sneer at "douchebags" using cellphones in public in the early 1990s, only to soon take pity on those who don't have the latest model, we are

likely looking at the future of online existence with immersive displays like Google Glass and Oculus Rift. Indeed, we can't be too far away from a future in which those people who make a living trying to stop you in the street to sign a petition, or contribute to a charity, hail you by name after matching your face with Google's database. ("What do you mean you can't talk today, you're in a hurry? According to your i-Calendar you still have forty minutes till your next appointment.")

17 When I used to wrestle with the elliptical machine at Ludlow Gym in New York's Lower East Side, my attention was often captured by a truck whizzing past the window on Delancey Street. I noticed this particular truck, as distinct from the hundreds of others, because it bore some spray-can graffiti on its side, which read: "This moment is punctuated by me and you." I often wondered who it was that created this message of delayed co-punctuation. But even without the shadow of a sense of who this person might be, my perception was impacted by them, and their decision to preemptively and virtually connect with others in this anonymous, "time-shifted" manner.

18 We might call this (realized) danger the "wikipedia-ization of knowledge": where concepts are no longer tested, produced, or adapted, but catalogued and contained, like dead butterflies pinned to a velvet board. "Knowing no longer involves using concepts," writes Lefebvre, "but simply receiving and memorizing information" (821). Further, "Substituted for knowledge, information deletes thought and reduces positive

knowledge to that which is amassed, accumulated, memorized without gaps, outside of lived experience" (822).

19 See Benjamin Fearnow, "Facebook Users Who Share Too Much Information More Lonely, Depressed." There are, however, alternative findings out there, such as a recent Pew study which notes that, according to their research, "overall, frequent internet and social media users do not have higher levels of stress. In fact, for women, the opposite is true for at least some digital technologies. Holding other factors constant, women who use Twitter, email and cellphone picture sharing report lower levels of stress" (Hampton et al.). Which is to say that the jury is out in this regard. Indeed, it probably always will be, given that the category of "social media" is so amorphous, and studies based on the scientific method are bound to be inconclusive, given the amount of different ways to interact online, the different strategies and demographics involved. It is tantamount to studying whether "using technology" makes one depressed or not: a question that cannot possibly come with a stable or definitive answer.

20 Adam Kramer et al., "Experimental Evidence of Massive-Scale Emotional Contagion through Social Networks."

21 Ibid.

22 See Laurie Penny, "It Can Manipulate Your Mood. It Can Affect Whether You Vote. When Do We Start to Worry?"

23 See Jonathan Zittrain, "Facebook Could Decide an Election Without Anyone Ever Finding Out."

24 See Brian Fung, "OkCupid Reveals It's Been Lying to Some of Its Users. Just To See What'll Happen."

25 See http://oktrends.okcupid.com/.

26 Charlie Chaplin is credited with saying, "Life is a tragedy when seen in close-up, but a comedy in long-shot." The lesson of big data is the reverse: an amusing bad date magnified a thousand times reveals the cynical and life-deadening calculations behind mass "emotional engineering."

27 During a heated exchange on Facebook, about the OK Cupid revelations, an ex-student of mine (who now works in the social media business) rhetorically asked, "Who said that your metadata belongs to you?!" before explaining to me, "That's how the internet works." What I found most disheartening about this line of thinking is the foreclosure on any alternative to technologies based on hypercapitalist business models: as if the Internet is, and always will be, like the laws of thermodynamics or a wankle-rotary engine. This is indeed how "the internet" works *right now*. But why is that? Because the 1 percent ensured that it would work precisely this way—as opposed to how it used to work, or how it could work in future, more in line with the interests of the commons or the multitude. As it is, all those tiny fans in our computers, whirring busily away, combine forces into a giant global updraft, sucking money toward the top echelons of society. And at much more than just our financial expense.

28 A social media quip, courtesy of Ed Keller.

29 See Ben Popper, "How the NYPD Is Using Social Media to Put Harlem Teens behind Bars." Concerning the

surveillance state, Derrida identifies the contemporary subject as enjoying "supervised liberty." Indeed, "which of us would dare to claim that we can escape it or even, which is more serious, that we want to escape it?" (310–11). For his part, Lyotard claims that modern democracy is "haunted by the suspicion that there is something that escapes [it], that might plot against [it]. [Democracy] need[s] the whole soul, and . . . need[s] this soul to surrender unconditionally" (118). Already seeing the forces which would coalesce in social media, Lyotard writes, "If you are not public, you disappear; if not exposed as much as possible, you don't exist. Your no-man's-land is interesting only if expressed and communicated. Heavy pressures are put on silence, to give birth to expression" (120). (With gratitude to Margret Grebowicz for drawing my attention to this insight of Lyotard.)

30 See Nick Fielding and Ian Cobain, "Revealed: US Spy Operation That Manipulates Social Media."

31 See Spencer Ackerman and James Ball, "NSA Performed Warrantless Searches on Americans' Calls and Emails."

32 See Matthew Phelan, "Amazon Is the Scariest Part of the CIA's New Amazon Cloud Storage."

33 For Barthes, idiorhythmy is not merely dancing to the beat of one's own drum, but "safeguarding *ruthmos*," which he defines as "a flexible, free, mobile rhythm; a transitory, fleeting form, but a form nonetheless" (35). This lends a kind of musicality to idiorhythmatic communities, which itself fosters a freeing and creative libidinal atmosphere. "The more idiorhythmy is foreclosed, the more Eros is excluded" (38)—an

observation we appreciate when indexed against our own often soul-deadening daily rhythms, so often dictated from elsewhere, but with which we are obliged to synchronize ourselves.

34 Barthes makes the very significant observation that most social theory works on the scale of the individual and/or the mass, but rarely focuses on mid-size groups, and the type of ethos and micro-politics that encourages or necessitates.

35 See Rob Horning, "Social Media Is Not Self-Expression."

36 Barthes's understanding of being together adds another dimension to the already depressing significance and relevance of Mike Judge's film *Idiocracy*, which satirically anticipates and depicts the accelerated unlearning and stupidity that haunts Stiegler's books, and the rest of us, in our daily lives.

37 In an interview with the *New Statesman*, McKenzie Wark identifies a new phase of this process, which he calls the Spectacle of Disintegration: "Partly in response to the events of May 1968 . . . the spectacle disintegrates and fragments, but doesn't go away. Social media and the internet made it microscopic— still centrally controlled, but diffuse, and reproduced and reiterated through fragments." For Wark's full account, see *The Spectacle of Disintegration: Situationist Passages Out of the Twentieth Century.*

38 See Jason Read, "Distracted by Attention."

39 Given the accelerating evolution of our species in accordance with our environment and our tools, we might speculate that humans will be the first species

to grow a third articulated limb for the sole purpose of taking selfies.

40 In passing, we might wonder about the new media's obsession with organic terms of combustion. If I hack my Kindle so that it can use Tinder, will I create my own Amazon Fire?

41 Stiegler himself describes hypersynchronization as a strategy or regime that "exhausts desire" (75), which in turn leads to the compulsive and profoundly anti-erotic situation that I have described elsewhere as "peak libido." See "The War on Terra" in my book *Human Error*, which engages in more detail with Stiegler's neo-Freudian argument.

42 By "auto-intoxication of the social," Grebowicz is relying on Baudrillard's notion of the masses as being the site of the "implosion of the social in the media." She quotes from Baudrillard's article on the same, which identifies the "redundancy of the social, this sort of continual voyeurism of the group in relation to itself: it must at all times know what it wants, know what it thinks, be told about its least needs, its least quivers, *see* itself continually on the videoscreen of statistics, constantly watch its own temperature chart, in a sort of hypochondriacal madness. The social becomes obsessed with itself; through this auto-information, this permanent autointoxication, it becomes its own vice, its own perversion" (*Masses* 210).

43 Perhaps the people have an inkling of this. Indeed, the pendulum seems to be swinging from the transparency of the now-classic reality TV show *Big Brother*—where the voyeuristic viewer could see through walls—to the

new British program called *Sex Box*, in which couples fornicate inside an opaque cube within the studio and then describe the encounter to a panel of "sexperts." This would suggest that we want to preserve an imaginative space, not colonized by the actuality of the image. In which case, such shows are about attempting to restore *the secret* within the harsh interrogation light of the panopticon. In other words, this is post-Snowden nookie.

44 For an amusing satirical take on this prevalent attitude and dilemma, see the *Portlandia* skit, "Social Bankruptcy," in which a woman goes to see a "Human Bandwidth Manager" to expunge all her social media contacts and obligations, only to realize the horror of being exiled, along with those Dantesque figures who prefer making scrapbooks with owl feathers to communicating on Facebook. The fact that these options are seen as such an extreme either/or scenario—drowning in digital solicitations, or being stranded with the marginals—says a great deal about the stark binaries with which we approach our world, now largely driven by planned obsolescence (of ways of thinking, as much as machines themselves).

45 See Kay Larson, "Signs and Symbols."

46 As one recent newspaper article notes: "Multitasking has been found to increase the production of the stress hormone cortisol as well as the fight-or-flight hormone adrenaline, which can overstimulate your brain and cause mental fog or scrambled thinking. Multitasking creates a dopamine-addiction feedback loop, effectively rewarding the brain for losing focus and for constantly searching for external stimulation. To make matters

worse, the prefrontal cortex has a novelty bias, meaning that its attention can be easily hijacked by something new—the proverbial shiny objects we use to entice infants, puppies, and kittens. The irony here for those of us who are trying to focus amid competing activities is clear: the very brain region we need to rely on for staying on task is easily distracted. . . . It is the ultimate empty-caloried brain candy. Instead of reaping the big rewards that come from sustained, focused effort, we instead reap empty rewards from completing a thousand little sugar-coated tasks." See Daniel J. Levitin, "Why the Modern World Is Bad for Your Brain."

47 The phrase "tertiary retentions" (or what Stiegler else-where calls *hypomnémata*) unfortunately conflates the various media in which we trust our outsourced memo-ries, whereby some forms of inscription (stone arrows, for instance) far outlast others (such as CDs, which we now know have trouble retaining their encoded information for more than twenty years). The fragil-ity of new media has prompted one of the "fathers of the Internet" and current Google vice president Vint Cerf to warn of a coming "digital dark age," in which "future generations will have little or no record of the 21st Century." There would indeed be some poetic justice in this, in which our strategy of planned obsolescence extended past our hardware, which can no longer read our mysterious messages, and into our global culture itself. See Pallab Ghosh, "Google's Vint Cerf Warns of 'Digital Dark Age.'"

48 To this assertion, the philosopher Simon Critchley reminds us of the classical distinction between

Gedächtnis and *Erinnerung*, "between an external, mechanized memory and an internal, living recollection." Thus, "what has happened," according to Critchley, "largely without anyone noticing it—is that we have outsourced memory onto the internet" (interview with Gallix). We might note, however, that a great deal of theorists have in fact noticed this, from McLuhan to Baudrillard to Stiegler to Agamben to Parikka to a host of lesser known writers working more explicitly with media and technology.

49 For a brilliant case study of pre-social media social engineering, which nevertheless has a strong overlap in terms of tricks, techniques, and motives, see Natasha Dow Schüll, *Addiction by Design: Machine Gambling in Las Vegas.* Regarding the depths to which online addiction can take us, see Valerie Veatch's remarkable documentary *Love Child* (2014), about a couple in South Korea who were so busy raising a virtual child online that they neglected to feed their actual baby, who subsequently died of malnutrition. See also Chris Baraniuk, "Inside an Internet Addiction Treatment Centre in China."

50 Courtesy of Drew Burk, publisher of the singular Univocal Press. The irony, of course, is not lost on any of us: the way we often post diatribes against Facebook *on* Facebook. Social media's capacity to amplify our disgust or impatience with social media is the very reason many of us find it impossible to "unplug" for any length of time. There is a shame-spiral involved with its use and abuse, just as there is with drugs and other forms of dependency.

51 Media theorist and activist Geert Lovink writes: "In the long post-war era from 1945 to 1989 the social became neutralized, and for the twenty-first century it returns as a special effect of technological procedures . . . and distinct from the community. The social lost its mysterious potential energy to burst suddenly onto the street and take power" (6).

52 One should always remember that the Luddites were not simply "against technology" because they felt an instinctive, romantic aversion to unnatural intruders, but rather because of the very specific reason that new industrial weaving machines were taking jobs and livelihoods.

53 For the German philosopher Peter Sloterdijk, the Internet and digital media do not represent a completely new paradigm, but are rather merely the latest iteration of older epistemological or ontological modes: "My assumption is that *there is nothing in technology that has not formerly been in metaphysics, and nothing in metaphysics that has not formerly been in magic.* Rationalization takes us from magic, to metaphysics, to technology. The metaphysics of man are condensed into technical devices. Networks are not satisfactory as models of the human, because networks can consist only of points and lines, and this is not enough to create a livable human form of life. Networks are anorexic tendencies that disenchant. That's why the notion of the human can add a spatial dimension to the notion of network." See the interview with Tom Boellstorff, "Satan at the Center and Double Rhizomes."

54 See Hito Steyerl, "The Spam of the Earth: Withdrawal from Representation."

55 Interestingly, Galloway, Thacker, and Wark make a claim for misguided attention in the rapidly evolving field of media studies itself, when they write, "Distracted by the tumult of concern around what media do or how media are built, have we not lost the central question: *what is mediation?*" (9).

56 We might call this the Jeremy England hypothesis, after the young physicist who has recently argued that life itself restructures itself to dissipate energy to avoid heat explosions. See Natalie Wolchover, "A New Physics Theory of Life." (Thanks to Sasha Litvinov for this analogy.)

57 Lovink provides one example of a call for deeper attention without resorting to pastoralist paradigms: "What we need are tools that no longer primarily focus on real-time and instead favor circumstances where counter-intuitive thought can occur. The perpetual state of distraction can be overcome by 'uncooling' and 'undesigning' the cult of multitasking and updating. The going offline movement will not be so anti-tech but anti-real-time. Technology will have to become our servant again. *How do we design in favor of attentive thought?*" (36, emphasis added).

58 What type of agenda exactly? One against the privatization of experience, as well as the corporate monopolization of violence, resources, representation, time, movement, technologies of production, reproduction, and interaction. For a start.

Works Cited

Ackerman, Spencer, and James Ball. "NSA Performed Warrantless Searches on Americans' Calls and Emails." *Guardian* (April 1, 2014). Online. http://www.the guardian.com/world/2014/apr/01/nsa-surveillance-loophole-americans-data.

Agamben, Giorgio. "What Is an Apparatus?" In *"What Is an Apparatus?" and Other Essays*. Translated by David Kishik and Stefan Pedatella. Stanford: Stanford University Press, 2009.

Badiou, Alain, with Nicolas Truong. *In Praise of Love*. Translated by Peter Bush. London: Serpent's Tail, 2012.

Bales, Kevin. *Disposable People: New Slavery in the Global Economy.* Berkeley: University of California Press, 2004.

Baraniuk, Chris. "Inside an Internet Addiction Treatment Centre." *New Scientist* (December 13, 2014). Online. http://www.newscientist.com/article/mg22429990.100-inside-an-internet-addiction-treatment-centre-in-china.html.

Barthes, Roland. *How to Live Together: Novelistic Simulations of Some Everyday Spaces*. Translated by Kate Briggs. New York: Columbia University Press, 2013.

Baudrillard, Jean. "The Ecstasy of Communication." In *The Anti-Aesthetic: Essays in Postmodern Culture*. Edited by Hal Foster. Port Townsend, WA: Bay Press, 1983.

———. *In the Shadow of the Silent Majorities . . . or The End of the Social, and Other Essays*. Translated by Paul Foss et al. New York: Semiotext(e), 1983.

———. "The Masses: The Implosion of the Social in Media." In *Selected Writings*. Edited by Mark Poster. Translated by Jacques Mourrain et al. Stanford: Stanford University Press, 1988.

———. *Revenge of the Crystal: Selected Writings on the Modern Object and Its Destiny, 1968–1983*. Translated by Paul Foss and Julian Pefanis. London: Pluto Press, 1999.

Bauman, Zygmunt. *Liquid Modernity*. Cambridge: Polity, 2000.

Beck, Taylor. "The Attention Machine." *Atlantic* (February 9, 2015). Online. http://www.theatlantic.com/technology/archive/2015/02/the-attention-machine/385284/.

Benjamin, Walter. *The Work of Art in the Age of Its Technological Reproducibility, and Other Writings on Media*. Edited by Michael W. Jennings et al. Cambridge, MA: Belknap Press, 2008.

Berardi, Franco. *Precarious Rhapsody: Semiocapitalism and the Pathologies of the Post-Alpha Generation*. New York: Minor Compositions, 2009.

Berlant, Lauren. "Faceless Book." *Berfrois* (December 20, 2014). Online. http://www.berfrois.com/2014/12/lauren-berlant-performs-clicking/.

WORKS CITED

Crary, Jonathan. *24/7: Late Capitalism and the Ends of Sleep*. London: Verso, 2014.

Critchley, Simon. Interviewed by Andrew Gallix. "Writing Outside Philosophy." *3AM Magazine* (December 3, 2014). Online. http://www.3ammagazine.com/3am/writing-outside-philosophy-an-interview-with-simon-critchley/.

Crogan, Patrick. "Thinking Cinema(tically) and the Industrial Temporal Object: Schemes and Technics of Experience in Bernard Stiegler's *Technics and Time* Series." *Scan*. Online. http://scan.net.au/scan/journal/display.php?journal_id=93.

Derrida, Jacques. *The Beast and the Sovereign: Volume 1*. Translated by Geoffrey Bennington. Chicago: University of Chicago Press, 2009.

Fearnow, Benjamin. "Facebook Users Who Share Too Much Information More Lonely, Depressed." *CBS News, Atlanta* (May 25, 2014). Online. http://atlanta.cbslocal.com/2014/05/25/study-facebook-users-who-share-too-much-information-more-lonely-depressed/.

Fielding, Nick, and Ian Cobain. "Revealed: US Spy Operation That Manipulates Social Media." *Guardian* (March 17, 2011). Online. http://www.theguardian.com/technology/2011/mar/17/us-spy-operation-social-networks.

Flusser, Vilém. *Post-History*. Translated by Rodrigo Maltez-Novaes. Minneapolis: Univocal, 2013.

Freud, Sigmund. *Civilization and Its Discontents*. Translated by James Strachey. New York: W. W. Norton, 2010.

Fromm, Erich. *The Art of Loving*. New York: Harper & Row, 1956.

Fung, Brian. "OkCupid Reveals It's Been Lying to Some of Its Users. Just To See What'll Happen." *Washington Post* (July 28, 2014). Online. http://www.washingtonpost.com/blogs/the-switch/wp/2014/07/28/okcupid-reveals-its-been-lying-to-some-of-its-users-just-to-see-whatll-happen.

Galloway, Alexander R., Eugene Thacker, and McKenzie Wark. *Excommunication: Three Inquiries in Media and Mediation.* Chicago: University of Chicago Press, 2014.

Ghosh, Pallab. "Google's Vint Cerf Warns of 'Digital Dark Age.'" *BBC News* (February 13, 2015). Online. http://www.bbc.com/news/science-environment-31450389.

Giroux, Henry A. *The Violence of Organized Forgetting: Thinking Beyond America's Disimagination Machine.* San Francisco: City Lights, 2014.

Grebowicz, Margret. *Why Internet Porn Matters.* Stanford: Stanford University Press, 2013.

Hampton, Keith, et al. "Social Media and the Cost of Caring." *Pew Research Center* (January 15, 2015). Online. http://www.pewinternet.org/2015/01/15/social-media-and-stress/.

Harman, Graham. *Guerrilla Metaphysics: Phenomenology and the Carpentry of Things.* Peru, IL: Open Court, 2005.

Harrison, Robert Pogue. "The Children of Silicon Valley." *New York Review of Books* (July 17, 2014). Online. http://www.nybooks.com/blogs/nyrblog/2014/jul/17/children-silicon-valley/.

Heidegger, Martin. "The Age of the World Picture." *The Question concerning Technology, and Other Essays.*

Translated by W. Lovitt. New York: Harper & Row, 1977.

Horning, Rob. "Social Media Is Not Self-Expression." *New Inquiry* (November 14, 2014). Online. http://the newinquiry.com/blogs/marginal-utility/social-media-is-not-self-expression/.

Johnson, Steven. *Everything Good Is Bad for You*. New York: Riverhead Books, 2006.

Kracauer, Siegfried. "The Cult of Distraction." *The Mass Ornament: Weimar Essays*. Translated and edited by Thomas Y. Levin. Cambridge, MA: Harvard University Press, 1995.

Kramer, Adam et al. "Experimental Evidence of Massive-Scale Emotional Contagion through Social Networks." *Proceedings of the National Academy of Sciences of the United States* (March 25, 2014). Online. http://www.pnas.org/content/111/24/8788.full.

Larson, Kay. "Signs and Symbols." *New York Magazine* (March 2, 1987), 96–99.

Lefebvre, Henri. *Critique of Everyday Life: The One-Volume Edition*. London: Verso, 2014.

Levitin, Daniel J. "Why the Modern World Is Bad for Your Brain." *Guardian* (January 18, 2015). Online. http://www.theguardian.com/science/2015/jan/18/modern-world-bad-for-brain-daniel-j-levitin-organized-mind-infor mation-overload.

Lovink, Geert. *Networks without a Cause: A Critique of Social Media*. Cambridge: Polity, 2011.

Lyotard, Jean-François. *Postmodern Fables*. Translated by Georges van den Abbeele. Minneapolis: University of Minnesota Press, 1997.

North, Paul. *The Problem of Distraction*. Stanford: Stanford University Press, 2012.

Pasquale, Frank. "The Algorithmic Self." *Hedgehog Review* 17, no. 1 (Spring 2015).

Penny, Laurie. "It Can Manipulate Your Mood. It Can Affect Whether You Vote. When Do We Start to Worry?" *New Statesman* (June 30, 2014). Online. http://www.new statesman.com/internet/2014/06/facebook-can-manipu late-your-mood-it-can-affect-whether-you-vote-when-do-we-start.

Pettman, Dominic. *Look at the Bunny: Totem, Taboo, Technology*. Winchester: Zero, 2012.

———. "The War on Terra." In *Human Error: Species-Being and Media Machines*. Minneapolis: University of Minnesota Press, 2011.

Phelan, Matthew. "Amazon Is the Scariest Part of the CIA's New Amazon Cloud Storage." *Black Box—Gawker* (July 21, 2014).

Plato. "The Symposium." *The Dialogues of Plato, Volume 1*. Translated by Benjamin Jowett. London: Macmillan, 1871.

Popper, Ben. "How the NYPD Is Using Social Media to Put Harlem Teens behind Bars." *Verge* (December 10, 2014). Online. http://www.theverge.com/2014/12/10/7341077/nypd-harlem-crews-social-media-rikers-prison.

Proust, Marcel. *The Captive*. Translated by C. K. Scott Moncrieff and Terence Kilmartin. New York: Modern Library Edition, 1993.

Read, Jason. "Distracted by Attention." *New Inquiry* (December 18, 2014). Online. http://thenewinquiry.com/essays/distracted-by-attention/.

Schüll, Natasha Dow. *Addiction by Design: Machine Gambling in Las Vegas.* Princeton, NJ: Princeton University Press, 2014.

Sloterdijk, Peter. "Satan at the Center and Double Rhizomes." Interview by Tom Boellstorff. *Los Angeles Review of Books* (January 14, 2014). Online. http://lareviewofbooks.org/interview/satan-center-double-rhizomes-discussing-spheres-beyond-peter-sloterdijk.

Standage, Tom. *Writing on the Wall: Social Media—The First 2,000 Years.* New York: Bloomsbury, 2013.

Steyerl, Hito. "The Spam of the Earth: Withdrawal from Representation." *e-flux*, 2012. Online. http://www.e-flux.com/journal/the-spam-of-the-earth/.

Stiegler, Bernard. *Acting Out.* Translated by David Barrison, Daniel Ross, and Patrick Crogan. Stanford: Stanford University Press, 2008.

———. "The Automatization of the Super-Ego and the Passage of Desire as Original Diversion of Libidinal Energy." In *The Lost Spirit of Capitalism: Disbelief and Discredit, volume 3.* Translated by Daniel Ross. Cambridge: Polity, 2014.

Turkle, Sherry. *Why We Expect More from Technology and Less from Each Other.* New York: Basic Books, 2012.

Vetö, Miklós. *The Religious Metaphysics of Simone Weil.* Albany: State University of New York Press, 1994.

Wark, McKenzie. *The Spectacle of Disintegration: Situationist Passages out of the Twentieth Century.* London: Verso, 2013.

———. "Spectacles of Disintegration." Interview by Juliet Jacques. *New Statesman* (May 16, 2013). Online. http://

www.newstatesman.com/culture/2013/05/spectacle-dis
integration.

Wolchover, Natalie. "A New Physics Theory of Life."
Scientific American (January 28, 2014). Online. http://
www.scientificamerican.com/article/a-new-physics-
theory-of-life/.

Zittrain, Jonathan. "Facebook Could Decide an Election
without Anyone Ever Finding Out." *New Statesman*
(June 3, 2014). Online. http://www.newstatesman.
com/politics/2014/06/facebook-could-decide-election-
without-anyone-ever-finding-out.

Žižek, Slavoj. "A Permanent Economic Emergency." *New
Left Review* 64 (July–August 2010).